SECOND EDITION

ABA Visualized Workbook

A visual workbook for learning behavior strategies

First published 2019, second edition 2023

ABA Visualized is a product of Studio van Diepen LLC

Copyright © Studio van Diepen LLC, 2023
The moral right of the authors has been asserted

Written by:
Morgan van Diepen

Design and Art Direction by:
Boudewijn van Diepen

Illustrations/Infographics by:
Boudewijn van Diepen, Saliha Caliskan

Edited by:
Rose M. Reynolds

www.ABAVisualized.com
info@ABAVisualized.com

ISBN: 978-0-578-64808-8

Printed in the USA by Lightning Source in a sustainable way

Contents

11 Instructions
12 The Power of Visuals

Foundations of ABA
22 Foundations of ABA
   Learning Objectives
24 Introduction
27 ABCs of Behavior
31 Functions of Behavior
40 Reinforcement/Punishment
46 Foundations of ABA Learning Check
48 Behavior Strategies
   Learning Objectives

Proactive Strategies
52 Altering the Environment
54 Priming
56 First, Then
58 Easy, Easy, Hard
60 Providing Choices
62 A Better Way to Say "No"

Reactive Strategies
66 Tell, Show, Help
68 Token Boards
70 A Note about Extinction
72 Extinction by Function
76 Extinction + Redirection
78 Blocking Unsafe Behaviors
80 Managing Self-injurious Behaviors
82 3 Reward Options

Teaching New Skills
86 Rapport Building
88 Personalized Teaching
90 Building Better Behaviors
92 Breaking Down Skills
94 Problem-Solving
96 Shaping & Fading
98 Modeling
100 Generalization
102 Play Skills
104 Joint Attention
106 Teaching to Request

Putting it all Together
110 Turning off Electronics
112 Improving On-task Behavior
114 Classroom Disruptions
116 Sharing Toys
118 Picky Eating
120 Following Directions
122 Transitions
124 Learning Personal Information
126 Encouraging Communication

Strategies for Inclusive Classrooms
130 Whole Class Reward System
132 Check-in, Check-out
134 Individual Points Plan
136 Behavior Strategies Learning Check

Visuals
139-213 Visuals that correspond with strategies

Note from the Authors

Our ABA Visualized Guidebook and Workbook were imagined and created out of a passion for supporting families and educators in learning effective strategies that will, in turn, improve their own children's and students' skills. While there are great behavior management resources available, our specific aim is to teach these strategies in a way that is easy to learn and easy to remember. By visualizing strategies that have been proven through research to be effective, we hope the concepts are now easily understandable and relatable to your individual needs. We hope this book gives you confidence as you practice each of the skills and support your child or learner's growth.

Thank you,
Morgan and Boudewijn van Diepen

About the Authors

Morgan van Diepen

Morgan is a Board Certified Behavior Analyst (BCBA) and Autism Specialist with over 15 years of working experience in Applied Behavior Analysis (ABA). Her work has been internationally recognized as a leader in disseminating behavior strategies in an engaging and approachable way. Through her presentations at respected conferences, custom trainings for organizations, and international experience working with families and schools, she continues to advocate for accessible behavioral expertise for families and teachers.

Bou van Diepen

Boudewijn (Bou) is an award-winning infographic designer who approaches every project from a conceptual and original perspective. His ability to effectively shape complex information into an understandable and aesthetically attractive visual is evidenced through his more than 10 years of diverse experience ranging from projects for government agencies to start-up nonprofit organizations. Boudewijn loves to use his creativity to make the world a more approachable place.

Our Mission

As an Applied Behavior Analysis (ABA) provider, I have had the opportunity to work with countless families, service providers, and educators over the years. I have heard a "nonverbal" child's first word, have helped an adult build his first friendship, and have seen individuals surpass skills they were told they could never do. Each little step of progress makes an impact not just on the individual and their family but also on me. Helping others to become more independent and more able to fully express themselves is tremendously rewarding. The mission of our company, ABA Visualized, is to make effective ABA strategies approachable, accessible, and relatable to all. We hope to support families and educators as they teach essential skills and promote learner independence. We aim to empower ABA providers such as BCBAs, RBTs, and behavior interventionists to have the skills and tools necessary to disseminate behavior expertise in an approachable and engaging way.

ABA Visualized has always been "for parents and teachers." Since its initial publication, we have seen an outpouring of testimonials from ABA providers who have expressed that this book has enabled them to better support families and educators in a meaningful way. This has been and will continue to be at the heart of everything we do. As we know through research and our own experiences, the more that families are involved in their child's skill development, the better the outcomes. While individuals can make great gains through their ABA sessions, the ones who make the most progress and sustain those skills over time are those who have families who are actively involved in their skill development. With the understanding of this crucial component, I searched for materials and teaching methods to most effectively involve families and educators. Most of what I found comprised of textual resources written with behavioral jargon or teaching methods involving verbally explaining and acting out strategies. I quickly realized the challenges with these teaching methods: families and educators often do not have time to read lengthy explanations of how to use a strategy or may not have access to a behavioral expert to model and explain each strategy to them. These challenges became more apparent while working with families from various backgrounds who use English as a second language. Understanding lengthy texts or even verbal instructions on how to do a strategy became laborsome and on some occasions, led to the strategies being learned incorrectly. It was through these experiences that my husband and co-author proposed a new way of teaching behavior strategies: through visuals.

By visualizing ABA strategies, we hope to bridge the gap between effective, yet technical, behavior expertise and those who could truly benefit from it on a daily basis: families and educators.

Instructions

This workbook is designed to be a supplemental product to our ABA Visualized Guidebook. In alignment with our vision to make ABA accessible, relatable, and approachable, we have created this workbook to assist those who teach behavior strategies to families, educators, and within their teams. We hope this customizable and interactive teaching style helps create an engaging and individualized learning experience!

How to use

The trainer should have the ABA Visualized Guidebook with them as the answer key, while each trainee should have their own workbook. The trainee (e.g., parent, caregiver, teacher, paraprofessional, ABA provider, etc.) will fill out the workbook as they complete the activities, making this a custom training tool!

The first chapter, "Foundations of ABA," proposes learning objectives based on the audience. Trainees will independently read about several core principles in Applied Behavior Analysis (ABA) and then practice applying the skills with the trainer. At the end of the chapter, you'll find a learning check to reflect on what has been learned.

The remaining chapters include evidence-based behavior strategies ready for you to fill out as you learn! It is intended that as the trainer teaches each strategy, the trainees will find the associated visuals to put together the step-by-step guide. This interactive learning method is recommended for staff trainings, parent trainings, and workshops!

Trainers should use the ABA Visualized Guidebook to help determine which strategies should be taught based on the team's priorities and needs. Before introducing the chosen strategy, cut out the corresponding visuals found in this workbook's "Visuals" section. As each strategy is taught, trainees should find the visuals representing each step. For example, the trainer may say, "the first step in priming is to provide a 1-minute or 5-minute warning of an upcoming transition." The trainees should then look through the visual deck to find the card that matches this step. The trainees should tape the visual with 1 piece of tape, allowing the visual to flap open or lay flat. As we have visualized each strategy through one real-life example, we encourage the trainee to write or illustrate their own example in the blank squares under the taped visual to make this resource more relatable.

The trainer and trainee can work together to write or draw in individualized examples of what each strategy would look like with their learner, or this could be assigned as an independent practice activity. These are our recommendations, but this is your workbook, so use it however is the most helpful to you!

The Power of Visuals

Visuals have long been known to amplify understanding, retention, and engagement when learning new skills. Within the fields of Applied Behavior Analysis (ABA) and Special Education, the positive influence of using visuals to support learners is widely accepted and celebrated. Visual supports have become indispensable tools in homes and classrooms. Yet, there's a noticeable gap in leveraging visual teaching when it comes to supporting parents, educators, and behavior support staff.

ABA Visualized is proud to be the first to take an innovative approach to teaching evidence-based behavior strategies through step-by-step visuals, making complex information more approachable, accessible, and relatable. Inspired by the many stories shared about the positive impact of visuals in behavior support, we are taking this work one step further by creating an online platform that makes behavior expertise accessible through visuals. BIP Visualized allows behavior professionals to create and customize their own visual behavior plans, access a growing library of visual strategies, resources, and on-demand trainings developed in collaboration with autistic consultants, and share everything directly with families, teachers, and behavior staff. This is the only platform built to support behavior planning, learning, and collaboration entirely through visuals.

With any of our new products, first comes a research deep dive to fully understand current barriers and experiences. In the following infographic, we're highlighting research findings comparing text-based learning with visual learning. We explore established multidisciplinary research on the efficacy of visuals versus text and reveal insights specific to the field of ABA. We've also been busy collecting our own research! With the recognized success of ABA Visualized's signature visual teaching style, we have been testing the impact of applying this approach to developing and disseminating Behavior Intervention Plans (BIPs). We're finding that teaching families and educators through text leads to low buy-in, low engagement, low understanding, and most importantly, low impact on the learner. Further, in our survey of over 200 behavior experts, only 35% reported feeling effective with their current teaching approach. Instead, when behavior strategies are taught through visuals, families and educators are more engaged, have better understanding, remember the skills longer, implement it more accurately, and feel more confident!

We're excited to share some of these findings with you, some of which may be eye-opening when considering their implications for the quality of services and care provided to our learners and their stakeholders. Our hope is that by highlighting the power of visuals, you will feel inspired to become a visual storyteller yourself!

Teaching with Text
The Traditional Way

Low Understanding

Text often leads to low understanding, which hinders parents' ability to advocate for their child's needs and potentially causes misinterpretation of recommended strategies.

(Banks et al., 2018; Critchfield et al., 2017)

Low Acceptance

The use of technical language in behavior recommendations can lead to reduced acceptance of the recommendations, particularly among individuals with little or no training in ABA principles. In fact, researchers found that people rate ABA jargon as "not motivating" and "unpleasant."

(Banks et al., 2018; Critchfield et al., 2017)

Low Engagement

Teaching through complex text can lead to low engagement because the team may struggle to follow behavior recommendations and resist change when the language is overly technical or hard to understand.

(Banks et al., 2018; Critchfield et al., 2017)

Low Accessibility

Text is not always accessible to everyone, as language barriers, especially for families with limited English proficiency, can hinder understanding and communication during behavior intervention discussions, leading to reduced parental engagement, misunderstandings, and increased stress and anxiety related to their child's needs.

(Andrade, Hancock, & Whaley, 2019; Bradshaw & Richey, 2015; Hatcher et al., 2016; Taylor & Landrum, 2016).

Low Confidence

Complex technical behavior recommendations can lead to low confidence as they often result in confusion, stress, and ineffective implementation, leaving stakeholders feeling unsupported and service providers ineffective.

In our own survey of people responsible for implementing behavior strategies, only 40% reported feeling confident and only 28% reported feeling prepared.

Feeling confident in using strategies

40%

Feeling prepared to support behaviors

28%

(Banks et al., 2018; Holt et al., 2016; Jarmolowicz et al., 2008; McMahon, Feldberg, & Ardoin, 2021).

Low Accuracy

Research shows that typical teaching approaches result in low accuracy with team members implementing less than 60% of the recommended strategies, and those being done so with an average accuracy rate of only 68%.

Parents & teachers report struggling to understand and implement complex technical instructions effectively.

Strategies implemented

60%

Accuracy of implemented strategies

68%

(de Bruin et al., 2014; Scheibel et al., 2022; Walker et al., 2021)

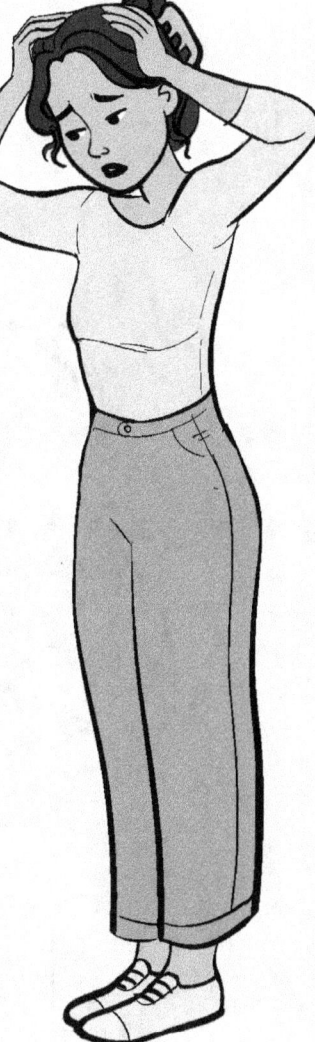

Low Collaboration

The use of technical language in behavior strategies often creates communication barriers, hindering effective collaboration between behavior specialists and stakeholders like parents and teachers.

In our own survey, only 25% of people responsible for implementing behavior strategies reported being aware of what strategies were being used in other settings.

(Peterson et al., 2018; Sailor & McCarthy, 2015)

Difficult to Remember

Text is easy to forget because our brain quickly loses information, we often overlook the middle parts of long texts, and dense material can overwhelm us.

In our pilot study, we found the average number of strategies included in a BIP was 26. However, the average number of strategies a person responsible for implementing could recall was only 3.

(The Forgetting Curve, Serial Position Effect, Cognitive Load Theory)

The Forgetting Curve for Text

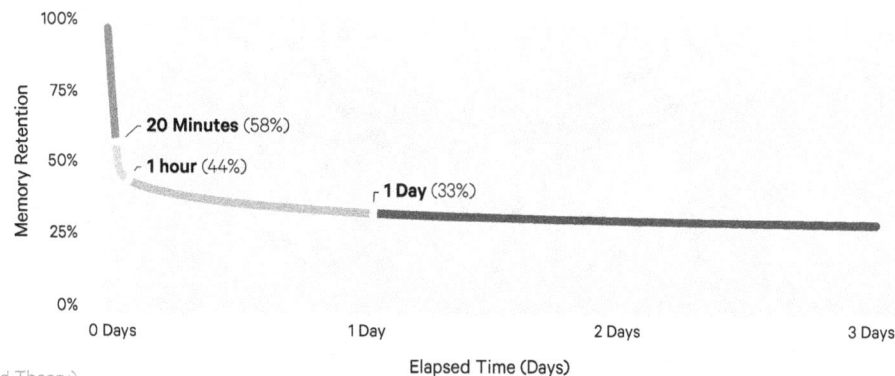

Teaching with Images
Our Innovative Approach

Better Understanding

Visuals make concepts easier to understand and they help teachers and parents better grasp behavior management strategies, making learning and skill application more effective.

(Albers & Greer, 2010; Eberhard, K., 2021; Hughes & Frederick, 2006; Sung-Hee, K., 2022).

More Preferred

Research has shown that most people overwhelmingly prefer and find instructions with visuals easier to use than traditional written instructions, indicating a clear preference for visuals over text-based content.

(Graff & Karsten, 2012).

More Engagement

Visuals improve engagement by capturing and holding the viewer's attention more effectively, as shown through eye-tracking studies. Visual storytelling makes the content more memorable and viewers engage longer.

(Harsh et al., 2019; HubSpot, 2022; Paradi, D., 1986).

More Accessible for Diverse Needs

Visuals offer greater accessibility, ensuring that those with diverse needs can access and understand the information.

(Abdulrahaman, et al., 2020).

Increased Confidence

Training with visual supports has been shown to boost confidence among parents and teachers in managing challenging behaviors.

(Clees & Brady, 2006).

Better Collaboration

The use of visuals has been shown to enhance communication between service providers, parents, teachers, fostering more effective collaboration in behavior management.

(Zarcone & Lindauer, 2006).

Higher Accuracy

Visuals significantly improve accuracy in comprehension, recall, and implementation. In one study, participants' accuracy in a behavior skill went from 38% to 99% when diagrams were added to the instructions, and accurate learning took less time!

Accuracy when taught with text

 38%

Accuracy when taught with visuals

 99%

Additionally, visual supports have been shown to improve educators' accuracy of implementing behavior strategies in both special education and general education classroom settings.

(Arco & Ricci, 2018; Graff & Karsten, 2012; Koegel & Koegel, 2006; Meyer & Bohning, 2011)

Better Retention

Using visuals alongside words makes information easier to remember because it engages different parts of the brain, reduces mental effort, and helps people see and remember relationships and patterns, ultimately improving retention.

Research has shown that people tend to remember information with visuals significantly better than text alone (65% compared to 10%), which is widely understood as "the picture superiority effect."

Remembering textual content

 10%

Remembering visual content

 65%

In our own pilot study, accurate recall improved by 57% when behavior strategies were presented as visuals instead of text.

(Dual Coding Theory, The Picture Superiority Effect, Cognitive Load Theory).

BIP Visualized

BIP Visualized is an online platform that makes behavior expertise more accessible through visuals. It supports behavior professionals in creating and customizing visual Behavior Intervention Plans while also providing a growing library of visual strategies, resources, and on demand trainings developed in collaboration with autistic consultants. All materials are designed to be shared directly with families, educators, and behavior staff.

While BIPs are well supported by research, many providers report challenges when plans are long, technical, or difficult for teams to understand and implement consistently. BIP Visualized replaces traditional text heavy approaches with step by step visual tools that are easier to learn, teach, and apply across settings. This visual approach supports clearer communication, stronger follow through, and more consistent support for learners at home, in schools, and in the community.

"As a seasoned BCBA, I can confidently say that BIP Visualized is a game-changer for the field of Applied Behavior Analysis"
Steven Camp, CEO at CAMP

"Please make this part of your toolbox of resources, you will not be disappointed!"
Shayla, School Psychologist at Fresno USD

"BIP Visualized is AMAZING!!! It's a lifesaver for BCBAs, a visual map for families, and filled with strategies everyone can use immediately."
Julia Bernasconi, BCBA

Try it out at **BIPVisualized.com**

How a Visual Behavior Plan Works

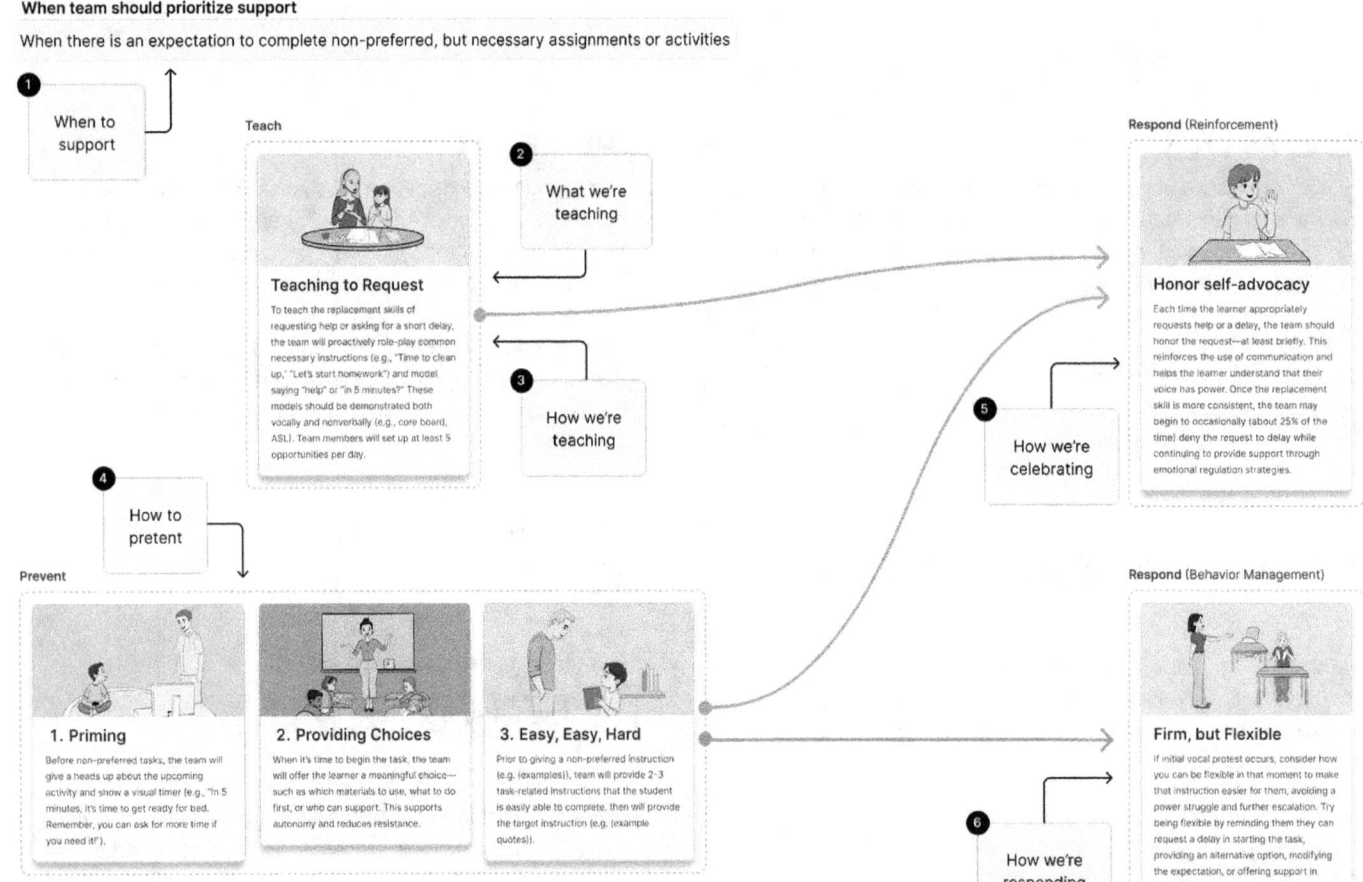

What Makes Us Different

 Save time without sacrificing quality

 Clear step-by-step visuals

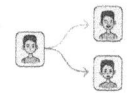 Focus on practical real-life applications

 Neurodiversity-affirming

 Unlimited sharing

 Trainings for the whole team

What You Can Do with BIP Visualized

Create Your Own Visual BIP
Go to "Create a visual BIP" and simply drag and drop evidence-based strategies to build a visual step-by-step plan for your team!

Features
~ Easy fill-in-the-blank descriptions
~ Fully customizable strategies
~ Print, download, or share
~ Real-time co-editing

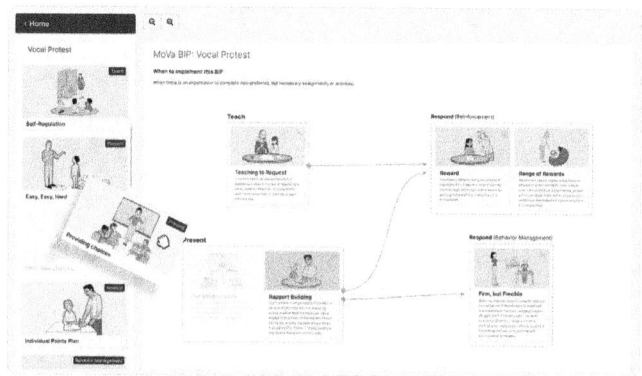

Edit and Customize Strategies
Edit strategies with your own images and text to make them completely individualized. Just click "Edit" on the top right of any strategy to customize!

Features
~ Upload images
~ Edit text
~ Save as template to reuse

Explore Courses and Resources to Share
Access a growing collection of trainings and resources to expand your own clinical expertise & support your team between sessions! Your account includes unlimited sharing, so your team can access everything you share—completely free.

We have trainings for
~ CEU trainings for BCBAs
~ Shareable trainings for educators
~ Shareable training for families

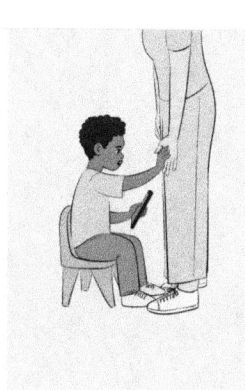

Foundations of ABA

Foundations of ABA Learning Objectives

For ABA providers and paraprofessionals
- Identify 3 of the core principles of Applied Behavior Analysis (ABA)
- Describe a client's behavior using observable, objective, and individualized language
- Collect at least 4 instances of ABC data on a client's target behavior
- Identify the function of a client's behavior based on ABC data
- Based on the determined function, propose 3 appropriate options for behavior strategies
- Collect baseline data on a client's target behavior
- Describe the difference between positive and negative reinforcement and provide an example of each for a current client
- Describe the difference between negative reinforcement and punishment
- Explain 3 tips for using reinforcement in approachable language as if speaking to a parent

For parents and caregivers
- Describe how the team will know if their recommendations are effective or if changes should be made
- Collect at least 4 instances of ABC data on the behavior of concern to help the team identify the "function" or why the behavior is occurring
- From the proposed options for behavior strategies, select which one you think would best support your child and aligns with your parenting values & style
- Collect baseline data on a client's target behavior
- Identify at least 3 items or activities that you think would be motivating for your child
- Through role-play or real life scenarios, demonstrate at least 2 tips for using reinforcement

For teachers
- Describe how the team will know if their recommendations are effective or if changes should be made
- Collect at least 4 instances of ABC data on the behavior of concern to help the team identify the "function" or why the behavior is occurring
- From the proposed options for behavior strategies, select which one you think would best support your child and aligns with your teaching values & style
- Collect baseline data on a student's target behavior
- Identify at least 3 items or activities that you think would be motivating for your student(s)
- Through role-play or real life scenarios, demonstrate at least 2 tips for using reinforcement

Introduction

In the following pages, we've selected text from our ABA Visualized Guidebook, which outlines foundational concepts within Applied Behavior Analysis (ABA). We recommend that those learning about behavior strategies independently read the text and then, together with the professional supporting them, complete the activities. It's not the goal for parents and educators to become experts on all the technical aspects of ABA, but rather on how to use effective behavior strategies to support their individual needs!

Introduction to ABA

Applied Behavior Analysis, or ABA, is a therapeutic approach that aims to improve the lives of individuals by teaching them meaningful skills that will help improve their independence. ABA was founded on several core principles that remain the foundation of the field today. These principles guide decision-making in which strategies should be used, how to best use them, and how to determine if they are effective. In approachable language, the principles of ABA can be summarized as choosing strategies that have been proven to be effective through research, applying them to daily life situations while maintaining their integrity, and continually analyzing results to determine if the strategies are making the intended behavior change or if revisions should be made.

Observable

ABA focuses on the observable aspects of behavior, meaning what we can see happening. We pay attention to what events occurred before and after the behavior to provide us clues as to why the behavior is occurring. It is believed that by assessing the environment and factors surrounding a behavior, we can begin to understand why the behavior is taking place; thus, we can begin to change it. In ABA, we look for reasons in the environment to explain why an individual engages in a behavior, rather than explaining the behavior through their feelings, mood, or even their diagnosis.

Observable, objective, individualized description of a behavior

Crying
Knees on ground
Hands in hair
Yelling

Upset
Angry
Having a bad day
Meltdown

A branch within ABA called Acceptance and Commitment Therapy (ACT) is pushing the boundaries past observable behavior a little bit! In this approach, there's an emphasis on considering "private events," including thoughts and feelings to better understand why behaviors occur. Practitioners still find ways to objectively define and measure these private events, staying true to ABA's core principles.

Objective

An essential part of practicing ABA is being objective. This starts from the beginning when we are first describing the behavior we want to change or the skill we want to teach. The word 'tantrum' likely creates a different image in different people's minds. Do you imagine the individual crying, screaming, lying on the ground, running away, saying 'no,' or any other behaviors? These are all observable and specific behaviors that we want to use when describing a goal to 'reduce tantrums.' Starting with describing a behavior in objective terms enables you to accurately track the progress of changing this behavior over time. It's also important to describe the behavior in a way that is clear to everyone: parents, teachers, and other care providers. Everyone on the team should understand what we mean when we say, "They had two tantrums today." Once you have created a clear description of the behavior you would like to change, you will learn how to collect data so you can determine if the strategies you are using are helping. The process of collecting data and assessing results is the objectiveness that makes ABA so effective. If the data shows we are not making progress toward our goal, we are able to recognize this and change approaches.

Individualized

Another essential factor of ABA is that strategies are adapted to meet the needs of each individual. We consider their strengths, preferences, and learning styles. In each visual strategy in this book, we've chosen a common scenario to teach the skill using step-by-step visuals. We encourage you to individualize the strategies by using them in situations that are most relevant to you and your learner. For example, in teaching the skill of requesting items, the individual may be expected to make a four-word request ("I want read book"), a one-word request ("book"), the ASL sign for "book," or use a Speech-Generating Device (also known as an AAC device) to press buttons of symbols or type out phrases to indicate they want to read a book. The steps of the strategy remain the same; however, the expectations may be altered to fit the learner's skill level and communication mode. Oftentimes, the best way to individualize your recommendations is to collaborate and consult with other professionals. In the previous example of teaching requesting skills, a Speech Language Pathologist (SLP) would be an essential team member in determining which communication method is most appropriate for a learner.

ABCs of Behavior

The ABCs of behavior is a way to determine why a behavior is happening. In ABA, the term 'behavior' refers to any observable action that a person can do. This encompasses not only challenging behaviors but all behaviors!

For many individuals receiving ABA services, there may be a challenging behavior the team would like to reduce. The first step in behavior reduction is understanding why the behavior occurs. To do this, you will need to attend to what is happening before (antecedent) and after (consequence) the behavior. Sometimes behaviors may feel like they're happening out of nowhere, but looking at the ABCs can help determine what's really causing them. Use the chart activity on the next page to help you become a behavior detective!

A
Antecedent
Events that occur immediately before a behavior

B
Behavior
An observable action

C
Consequence
Events that occur immediately after a behavior

ABCs at home example
- Antecedent: Mother tells child to get their shoes
- Behavior: Child screams
- Consequence: Mother gets the shoes herself

ABCs at school example
- Antecedent: Teacher asks students a question
- Behavior: Student raises hand
- Consequence: Teacher calls on student

Instructions for filling out ABC Chart

1. Choose one behavior to target (e.g. yelling, vocal protest, hitting, etc.). Include a description of what this behavior looks like for this learner.
2. Every time this behavior occurs, fill out the chart with (A) what happened immediately prior, (B) what the behavior looked like, (C) what happened immediately afterward/how you responded.
3. Optional: Add comments with more information about what was happening at that time (e.g. in the store, in the car, during bedtime routine, did/did not take medication this day).
4. Record information for at least four times the behavior occurs (can all be during one day if the behavior occurs a lot, or can be over several days if the behavior does not occur as often).

ABC Chart Example

Target Behavior: Tantrum (Yelling, crying, falling to the ground)

Antecedent What happened before the behavior?	Behavior Describe the behavior	Consequence What happened after the behavior?	Function
Mom told son to "turn off iPad"	Yelled, "no, no, no," and cried for 2 minutes	Mom took iPad	
Son asked Mom, "can I watch cartoons?" + Mom said, "not right now"	Fell on ground, yelled, "I want cartoons!" cried for 3 minutes	Mom told son to stop yelling	
Son was watching *Super Wings* with family	Yelled, "I want Mickey Mouse!" fell to ground	Mom changed channel to Mickey Mouse	
Son asked Mom to buy chocolate cereal, Mom said, "no"	Fell on ground, cried for 1 minute	Mom picked up son and put in shopping cart	

Your turn!

Choose a specific behavior to target. Describe that behavior using observable and objective words ("Target Behavior"). Fill out the chart below for the next four times that behavior occurs.

Note: Sometimes, a consequence is also the antecedent for the next behavior.
Example: (A) Instruction to do homework (B) learner yells (C) teacher repeats the instruction to do homework // (A) teacher repeats the instruction to do homework (B) learner rips paper (C) teacher tapes paper and repeats the instruction.

You can leave the function column blank for now.

ABC Chart

Target Behavior:

Antecedent What happened before the behavior?	**Behavior** Describe the behavior	**Consequence** What happened after the behavior?	**Function**

More practice

Choose a specific behavior to target. Describe that behavior using observable and objective words ("Target Behavior"). Fill out the chart below for the next four times that behavior occurs.

ABC Chart

Target Behavior:

Antecedent What happened before the behavior?	Behavior Describe the behavior	Consequence What happened after the behavior?	Function

Functions of Behavior

The functions of behavior refer to the reason someone is engaging in a behavior. Understanding the 'why' is essential when aiming to change that behavior because it enables us to address the cause, instead of just focusing on stopping the behavior. While reducing challenging behaviors is a common goal that ABA can support, the actual focus should be on finding better ways for learners to express themselves and self-regulate. Research shows that building these replacement skills is the most effective way at reducing challenging behaviors. But in order to know which replacement skill to teach, we need to know the function.

If an individual disrupts the classroom by frequently getting out of their seat to pace around the room, before we decide how to manage that behavior, we need to know why it is occurring. They could be trying to escape the work, trying to make their friends laugh, or just feeling the need to stretch their legs—we don't know someone's intentions, but we can look for patterns to help us understand! This initial understanding that behaviors happen for a reason will lead to more success in behavior management. In the field of Applied Behavioral Analysis, it is believed that there are four functions, or reasons, that behavior may occur. You can remember them as let's "SEAA why a behavior is happening."

1. **Sensory** (an internal/external sensation or self-regulation)
2. **Escape** (from a demand or situation)
3. **Access** (to an item, activity, or the way something is done)
4. **Attention** (from others)

An important note is that while in ABA, we look for patterns that help us determine why a behavior is occurring (its function), sometimes there are outside factors (setting events) influencing a behavior. This could include pain, medication, sleep, or other biological reasons. Within ABA, we are also understanding that thoughts and feelings (private events) also influence a person's behavior, although that is harder to track and measure. Once you have ruled out any medical reasons for the behavior, you can start to determine why the behavior is occurring and create an individualized plan to teach skills that meet these same needs. In ABA jargon, this is called teaching a "functionally-equivalent replacement behavior." In the previous example about a learner who paces around the classroom, we will need to determine: Is he gaining attention from the teacher/peers? Is he walking around the room so he can access some preferred items? Is the walking delaying or preventing him from completing an assigned task? Or is it fulfilling a sensory need for movement? We can determine the function of the behavior by looking at the ABCs. Use the ABC template to record at least four occurrences of the target behavior and the ABCs surrounding that behavior. With this information, we can look for patterns to choose which function is the likely reason the behavior is occurring. In the next illustrations, we will examine how one behavior could occur for four different reasons and how to determine the cause. The example behavior shown is a learner engaging in the self-injurious behavior (SIB) of hitting himself on the head.

Clues that the behavior is Attention function

- The individual was previously receiving attention from someone, and then that person stopped giving attention just before the target behavior occurred.
- Immediately after the target behavior, someone gave the individual attention. Remember that reprimands (e.g. "no," "don't do that") are also a form of attention.

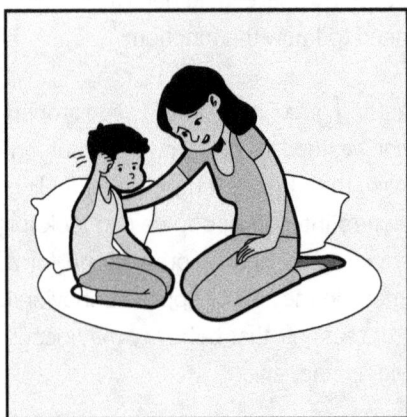

The individual receives attention after he engages in the behavior.

Here, following the SIB, the teacher is giving attention by comforting the learner. Remember, reprimands ("don't do that," "stop," "no") are also forms of giving attention.

Clues that the behavior is Access function

- A preferred item or activity was taken away from the individual just before the target behavior occurred.
- The individual was told "no," "not right now," or "wait."
- Immediately after the target behavior, someone gave the individual a preferred item or activity.

The individual engages in the target behavior after being told "no," "not right now," or "wait."

Here, the learner asked for the phone and was told "no" immediately prior to the SIB.

Clues that the behavior is Escape function
- The individual was instructed to complete a task just before the target behavior occurred.
- Immediately after the target behavior, the expectation to complete a task was removed.

Following the target behavior, the individual is able to escape from a non-preferred task.

Here, following the SIB, the teacher is allowing the learner to escape his work task by going to a quiet area to "calm down."

Clues that the behavior is Sensory function
- The behavior occurred when the individual was alone and no tasks were given.
- The behavior occurs across all people, settings, and activities.

Note: Some learners may engage in sensory behaviors as an expression of their emotions or a way to self-regulate. As long as these behaviors are not causing harm or impeding learning, there is no need to aim to reduce them.

The individual is engaging in the behavior because it "feels good" or helps them self-regulate.

When the function is sensory, the learner does not need the teacher in order to have reinforcement.

Once you are able to identify the function of the behavior, you are ready to move on to learning strategies that reduce this challenging behavior!

Identifying the function

Next, you will use the information you collected in columns A, B, and C as clues to make the best guess at which of the four functions is the reason the behavior is happening. You can circle the most important clue from each row to help guide your decision.

ABC Chart Example

Target Behavior: Tantrum: Yelling, crying, and falling to the ground

Antecedent What happened before the behavior?	Behavior Describe the behavior	Consequence What happened after the behavior?	Function
Mom told son to "turn off iPad"	yelled, "no, no, no" and cried for 2 minutes	Mom took iPad	Access (iPad)
Son asked Mom, "can I watch cartoons?" + Mom said, "not right now"	Fell to ground, yelled, "I want cartoons!" cried for 3 minutes	Mom told son to stop yelling	Access (watching cartoons)
Son was watching *Super Wings* with family	Yelled, "I want Mickey Mouse!" fell to ground	Mom changed channel to Mickey Mouse	Access (watching Mickey Mouse)
Son asked Mom to buy chocolate cereal, Mom said "no"	Fell to ground, cried for 1 minute	Mom picked up son and put in shopping cart	Access (chocolate cereal)

Function: Access

Your turn!

Fill out the chart below for the next four times the target behavior occurs. Look for clues to what is happening before or after the behavior. Use these clues to determine the function for each time the behavior occurred, and then identify which was the most common.

Go back to your previous ABC data. Which of the four functions is being observed in each occurrence of the target behavior? Or which function is occurring the most? Some behaviors may be controlled by multiple functions, meaning the individual may be engaging in the behavior for several reasons. Look to see which occurs most often and start there!

ABC Chart

Target Behavior:

| Antecedent
What happened before the behavior? | Behavior
Describe the behavior | Consequence
What happened after the behavior? | Function |
|---|---|---|---|
| | | | |
| | | | |
| | | | |
| | | | |

Function: _____

Alternative option: ABC Checklist

Instructions for filling out ABC Checklist: Fill this out every time you see the target behavior occur by checking off the boxes that relate to the particular incident. This may help you to identify if any patterns are occurring or observe why the behavior is happening.

A note for providers: This checklist version may be easier for families or educators. You could also fold back the function column and complete that section yourself.

ABC Chart

Target Behavior: _____

Antecedent What happened before the behavior?	**Behavior** Describe the behavior	**Consequence** What happened after the behavior?	**Function**
☐ Was told "no" ☐ Was asked to do something ☐ Attention given to others ☐ Transition ☐ Nothing "out of the blue"	☐ Cries ☐ Hits ☐ Screams ☐ Throws object ☐ --------------	☐ Redirected to alternative behavior ☐ Told "no" ☐ Given what s/he wants ☐ Ignored ☐ Verbal reprimand	☐ Attention ☐ Access ☐ Escape ☐ Sensory
☐ Was told "no" ☐ Was asked to do something ☐ Attention given to others ☐ Transition ☐ Nothing "out of the blue"	☐ Cries ☐ Hits ☐ Screams ☐ Throws object ☐ --------------	☐ Redirected to alternative behavior ☐ Told "no" ☐ Given what s/he wants ☐ Ignored ☐ Verbal reprimand	☐ Attention ☐ Access ☐ Escape ☐ Sensory
☐ Was told "no" ☐ Was asked to do something ☐ Attention given to others ☐ Transition ☐ Nothing "out of the blue"	☐ Cries ☐ Hits ☐ Screams ☐ Throws object ☐ --------------	☐ Redirected to alternative behavior ☐ Told "no" ☐ Given what s/he wants ☐ Ignored ☐ Verbal reprimand	☐ Attention ☐ Access ☐ Escape ☐ Sensory

Function: _____

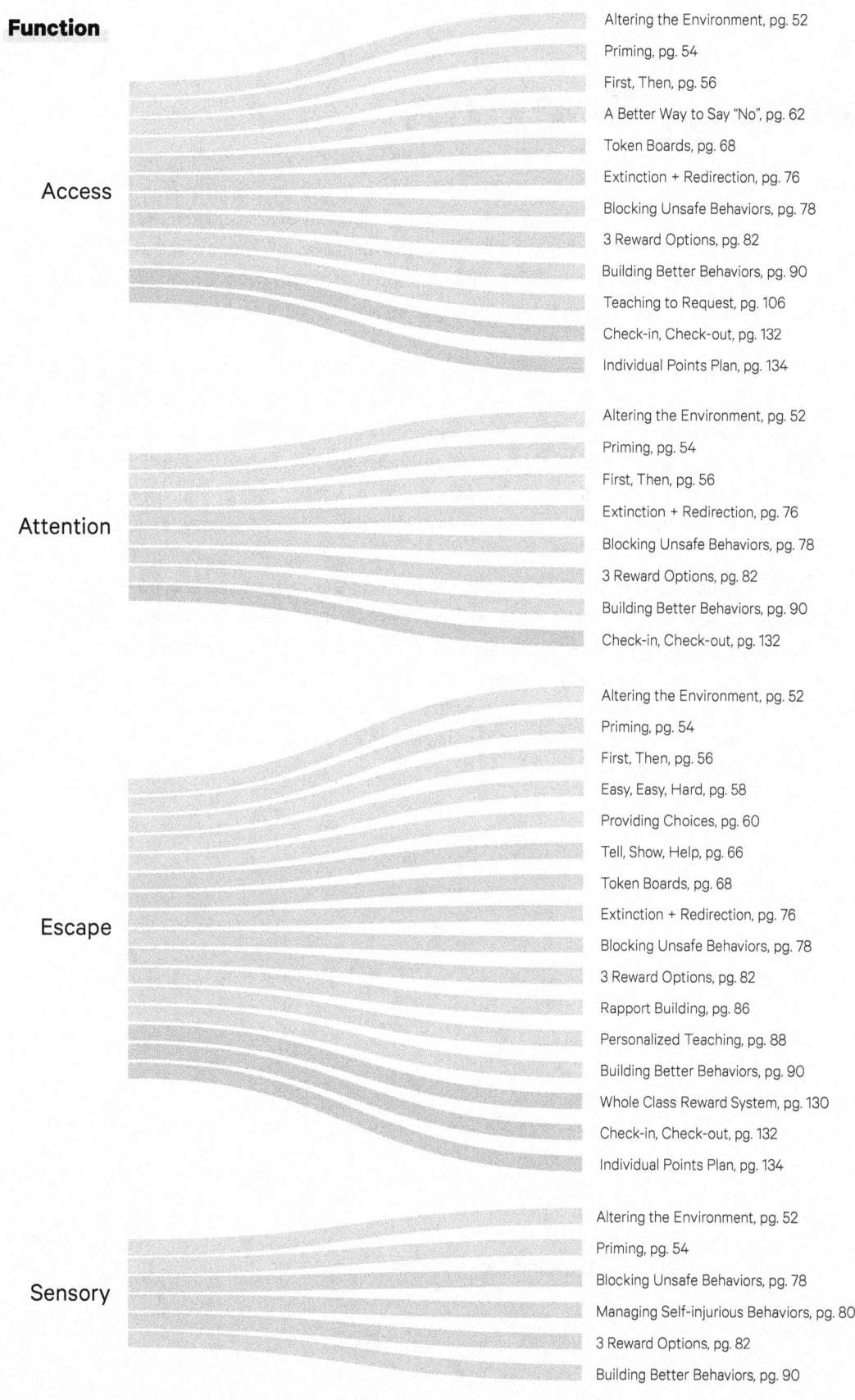

Data Collection

An integral part of using ABA strategies is having a reliable way of measuring if the strategies are effective. Although there are many different means of collecting data to measure behavior, the essential elements include understanding why and how often a behavior occurs. The ABC Data you have already collected provides insight into why a behavior is happening.

Before learning any behavior strategies, trainees should collect "frequency data," which is just a count of how often the target behavior occurred that day. The frequency of the behavior before introducing any strategies can be called the "baseline." We recommend collecting at least three days of baseline data. As the strategies are introduced, trainees should monitor changes in frequency of the behavior to determine if the strategies are working to help reduce the behavior of concern. We recommend adding a note on the date column when introducing a new strategy.

Note: The strategies featured in the following chapters have all shown to be effective; however, as behavior is developed from a pattern of experiences, it is important to remember that behavior change does not often occur immediately. The best way to utilize the strategies to create impactful behavior change and see results is to be consistent. Once you've identified a strategy that works well for your learner (the frequency of a concerning behavior is decreasing or has reached zero!), expand on how you could use that strategy to build other skills or help in other challenging situations.

Target behavior: _____

Date	Frequency

Reinforcement/Punishment

In ABA, reinforcement and punishment are understood as the factors that can change our behaviors over time. This is built on B.F. Skinner's research on behavior which determined that behavior can be taught or changed by changing what happens after the behavior (the consequence). Remember that in ABA, consequence just means something that happens after a behavior—it's not necessarily "good" or "bad." In short, reinforcement is something that makes the behavior likely to occur more in the future, and punishment is something that makes the behavior likely to occur less in the future. It is important that we understand whether our responses to an individual's behavior are actually reinforcing (increasing) or punishing (decreasing) that behavior.

Example
- A student is talking out in class during math. The teacher sends the student to the hallway. The student liked being in the hallway because he didn't have to do math. In the future, he will talk out during math again (his behavior was increased, or reinforced).
- A student is talking out in class during math. The teacher sends the student to the hallway. The student became embarrassed that he had to leave the class in front of his friends. In the future, he will not talk out during math (his behavior was decreased, or punished).

In this example, the teacher's response (consequence) of sending the student to the hallway led to different future results, even if she had the same intent in both scenarios. By understanding how our responses change our learners' behaviors, we are able to be more intentional about how we respond. If we learn that receiving praise is reinforcing for an individual, we can give praise after he completes a task and expect that he will likely try that task again in the future. But not everyone likes praise! We first need to evaluate what actually happens to the behavior we are praising—does it increase or decrease? Alternatively, if we know that taking away electronics is punishing for an individual, we can take away electronics after he engages in a challenging behavior and expect that he will be less likely to engage in that challenging behavior in the future. If taking away electronics is meaningless to the individual, it's not actually punishing the behavior after all. Although reinforcement and punishment are both impactful in changing behavior, in ABA, we heavily focus on reinforcement and only utilize punishment when reinforcement is not showing meaningful progress. There are negative side effects to using punishment, but most importantly, punishment only aims to decrease a behavior. It does not teach the individual what behaviors they should do instead. In ABA, even when we are aiming to decrease a behavior, we actually do this by focusing on skill-building. This is how you can create more impactful, long-lasting behavior change.

Types of reinforcement

To look more in-depth at how reinforcement works, we must first understand the two types: positive reinforcement and negative reinforcement.

Positive reinforcement

Positive reinforcement simply means something is given, which makes the behavior more likely to occur in the future.

Common types of positive reinforcement

- Giving praise, compliments
- Giving high fives, tickles, smiling at the person
- Giving money
- Giving access to toys/electronics
- Giving preferred foods

Example: You do the dishes before your partner comes home from work. When your partner sees the clean dishes, he gives you a kiss and says 'thank you.' In the future, when you are home before your partner, you will be more likely to do the dishes. (The partner gave a kiss and praise, and you continued to do the dishes more often, so this is positive reinforcement.)

While many people enjoy receiving compliments and recognition, not everyone does. Before giving praise for all those exciting moments of progress with your learner, determine if this is actually reinforcing for them, meaning, your celebrations are motivating them to do that behavior or skill more often. If your learner does not like praise, try giving points or tokens that they can exchange later for a favorite item or activity instead. You can also try giving more discrete recognition like a thumbs up from across the room.

By giving something preferred following a behavior, that behavior will be more likely to occur in the future.

Here, the teacher is giving praise and a sticker following the learner's on-task behavior. Because the teacher has done this before, she knows he is likely to continue being on-task to earn more praise and stickers.

Negative reinforcement
Negative reinforcement means something is taken away, which makes the behavior more likely to occur in the future.

Common types of negative reinforcement
- Removing aversive noises
- Removing pain
- Removing annoying situations
- Removing aversive tasks

Example: You are leisurely driving on the highway and a car is honking loudly behind you. You move lanes and let the car pass. You continue to do this throughout your relaxing drive anytime someone honks behind you. (By moving lanes, the car honking stopped, <u>removing</u> an aversive sound. You <u>continued</u> to do this behavior. Removing & continuing = <u>negative</u> reinforcement.)

By removing something non-preferred following a behavior, that behavior will be more likely to occur in the future.

Here, the teacher is removing the work task following the learner's on-task behavior, giving him a break from the task. Because the teacher has done this before, she knows he is likely to continue being on-task the next time work is presented so that he can earn more breaks.

As these are both still reinforcement, the behavior will be more likely to occur in the future, whether something was added or taken away.

What's the difference between negative reinforcement and punishment?
To be "reinforcement," we know that the behavior will be more likely to occur in the future. Remember that the "negative" indicates that something was taken away, rather than the common understanding that negative = bad. Thus, negative reinforcement means that following a behavior, something was taken away, which will make that behavior more likely to occur in the future. Punishment, rather, indicates that a behavior will be less likely to occur in the future.

Tips for using reinforcement

Reinforcement shapes how we behave, and for this reason, is the core of all ABA strategies. There are several factors which make reinforcement even more effective by leading to faster and/or more sustaining desired change.

Reinforcement should be motivating

Identifying motivation is key to the success of any behavior change program. What we find motivating or rewarding is different for everyone, and this can change daily! Before starting to teach your learner any new skills, first identify what they may be motivated to earn as rewards for making progress towards those goals. You may be able to simply ask some learners, but for others, you may need a more structured approach.

Before starting to teach any new skills, identify what could potentially be motivating for the learner to earn. Place a few preferred items around the room and watch which items naturally draw the learner's attention. This is a quick and easy way to determine what may be motivating in that moment. Also, consider your learner's special interests! Getting to spend time researching topics they love could be very motivating for many learners.

Reinforcement should be immediate

For the learner to learn what they did was correct, the reinforcement should immediately follow the behavior. It is less likely that you will see the behavior increase if you give a delayed reward. For example, if a learner appropriately requests play-doh, but you give the play-doh 15 minutes later, he might not associate the request with earning the play-doh.

First, determine what is most motivating for the learner. Is it: praise, a break from a task, playing with an item/activity, or earning points towards a bigger reward? When teaching a new skill and the learner does it independently, recognize and celebrate it by giving that reward right away!

Reinforcement should match effort

Consider the difficulty of the task when deciding how much reinforcement to give. The size of the reinforcer needs to fit the size of the effort. For example, if you have to provide a lot of assistance while your learner is putting on their shoes, you may give a little praise at the end (e.g. 'nice job pulling tight'); however, if they tie their shoes on their own, you will want to give a lot of praise and possibly an extra reinforcer (like more time playing outside) to celebrate. Save the big rewards and big excitements for the harder skills that your learner is working to learn!

The more effort the learner puts in, the more reinforcement they should get.

Here, the teacher needed to support the learner a lot with tying his shoes, so she gave a little praise.

If he did a new step of tying shoes for the first time on his own, she should show a lot more excitement (e.g. high fives, cheers, etc.).

Provide choices of reinforcers

Before giving a difficult instruction, ask the learner what they would like to work for. For many learners, it's beneficial to physically show two or three choices of activities/items that can be earned. Remember to follow through with giving that item immediately when the learner finishes the task.

Prior to giving a demand, provide 2-3 choices of activities/items than can be earned. Use the specific item chosen as the reinforcer to motivate the learner to complete the instruction.

Limit access to reinforcers

In order to keep motivation high, it is recommended to save the reinforcers for those teaching moments. If learners have access all the time to their favorite toys, activities, and food, they will be less motivated to work for these items. This may include physically putting away preferred items or limiting time on electronics. Rotate the items so that the learner will maintain interest in a variety of items and activities and stay motivated to work for them.

Place preferred items in boxes or on a shelf that is out of reach. Limit access to these items in order to keep them motivating for those teaching moments. A learner who has limited access to a favorite toy will be more motivated to work to earn it compared to a learner who has free access to this toy throughout the day. We want to keep the rewards feeling special and motivating!

Fade reinforcement when skill is learned

When learning a new skill, we want to celebrate every step of progress along the way. As the learner begins to improve and do more of the skill independently, continue to recognize this progress, but start shifting to building "intrinsic motivation," where instead of working for praise and prizes, they just feel proud of what they've accomplished. Try saying things like, "You did that on your own! I bet you feel so proud!" or "You took care of yourself when you felt angry; you should be proud of yourself!" As they're learning a new skill, celebrate their independence, even if they make a few mistakes along the way.

For new skills: celebrate every attempt and every step in progressing towards independence. Once they have learned to do the skill on their own: fade out the amount of praise and reinforcement you are giving. To help encourage that intrinsic motivation and pride, start shifting your language from "I love that you dressed yourself!" to "You should feel proud that you did that all by yourself!"

Foundations of ABA Learning Check

For ABA providers and paraprofessionals

- [ ] Identify 3 of the core principles of Applied Behavior Analysis (ABA)
- [ ] Describe a client's behavior using observable, objective, and individualized language
- [ ] Collect at least 4 instances of ABC data on a client's target behavior
- [ ] Identify the function of a client's behavior based on ABC data
- [ ] Based on the determined function, propose 3 appropriate options for behavior strategies
- [ ] Collect baseline data on a client's target behavior
- [ ] Describe the difference between positive and negative reinforcement and provide an example of each for a current client
- [ ] Describe the difference between negative reinforcement and punishment
- [ ] Explain 3 tips for using reinforcement in approachable language as if speaking to a parent

For parents and caregivers

- [ ] Describe how the team will know if their recommendations are effective or if changes should be made
- [ ] Collect at least 4 instances of ABC data on the behavior of concern to help the team identify the "function" or why the behavior is occurring
- [ ] From the proposed options for behavior strategies, select which one you think would best support your child and aligns with your parenting values & style
- [ ] Collect baseline data on a client's target behavior
- [ ] Identify at least 3 items or activities that you think would be motivating for your child
- [ ] Through role-play or real life scenarios, demonstrate at least 2 tips for using reinforcement

For teachers

- [ ] Describe how the team will know if their recommendations are effective or if changes should be made
- [ ] Collect at least 4 instances of ABC data on the behavior of concern to help the team identify the "function" or why the behavior is occurring
- [ ] From the proposed options for behavior strategies, select which one you think would best support your child and aligns with your teaching values & style
- [ ] Collect baseline data on a student's target behavior
- [ ] Identify at least 3 items or activities that you think would be motivating for your student(s)
- [ ] Through role-play or real life scenarios, demonstrate at least 2 tips for using reinforcement

Behavior Strategies Learning Objectives

For ABA providers and paraprofessionals

- Describe and demonstrate 3 proactive strategies using approachable language, including the goal, how, and context as it relates to a specific client
- Describe and demonstrate 2 strategies for responding to challenging behaviors using approachable language, including the goal, how, and context as it relates to a specific client
- Describe and demonstrate 2 strategies for reinforcing appropriate behaviors using approachable language, including the goal, how, and context as it relates to a specific client
- When provided a client-specific scenario, explain and demonstrate what Extinction + Redirection would look like and why this is more ethical than implementing Extinction alone
- Describe and demonstrate 2 options for differential reinforcement using approachable language, including the goal, how, and context as it relates to a specific client
- Demonstrate demand-free, child-led play for 5 minutes with a client (Rapport Building strategy)
- When provided a client's skill acquisition goal, explain how this skill could be taught using Personalized Teaching considering the client's interests and strengths
- Describe and demonstrate functional communication training (Building Better Behaviors, Teaching to Request strategies, Expanding Communication) using approachable language, including the goal, how, and context as it relates to a specific client
- Demonstrate supporting a client with a daily living skill through a provided task analysis, showing understanding of various prompting techniques (Breaking Down Skills strategy)
- Describe the difference between Shaping and Fading using skill acquisition goals specific to a client
- Describe 3 ways to promote generalization
- When provided with a client's Behavior Intervention Plan (BIP), demonstrate each strategy during role-play, then with the client (Putting it all Together)
- When provided with an inclusive classroom strategy, describe how you could support the teacher in implementing the plan

For parents and caregivers

- After being taught a proactive strategy specific to your family, describe and demonstrate the strategy with your child
- After being taught a strategy for responding to challenging behaviors specific to your family, describe and demonstrate the strategy with your child
- After being taught a strategy for recognizing and rewarding appropriate behaviors specific to your family, describe and demonstrate the strategy with your child
- Demonstrate demand-free, child-led play for 5 minutes (Rapport Building strategy)
- Demonstrate how to proactively teach communication with your child (Building Better Behaviors, Teaching to Request strategies, Expanding Communication)

- Demonstrate supporting your child with a daily living skill through a provided task analysis
- For a specific scenario that is challenging for your child, demonstrate each strategy during role-play, then with your child (Putting it all Together)

For teachers

- After being taught a proactive strategy specific to your classroom, demonstrate the strategy with your students
- After being taught a strategy for responding to challenging behaviors specific to your classroom, demonstrate the strategy with your students
- After being taught a strategy for recognizing and rewarding appropriate behaviors specific to your classroom, demonstrate the strategy with your students
- Demonstrate demand-free, child-led play for 5 minutes with a student (Rapport Building strategy)
- Demonstrate how to proactively teach communication with a student (Building Better Behaviors, Teaching to Request strategies, Expanding Communication)
- For a specific scenario that is challenging for a student, demonstrate each strategy during role-play, then with the student (Putting it all Together)
- In collaboration with the trainer, explain how to set up and implement a Whole Class Reward System that aligns with your classroom needs
- In collaboration with the trainer, explain how to set up and implement either the Check-in, Check-out or Individual Points Plan strategy for a specific student

Proactive Strategies

Altering the Environment

Changing the setting to set up the learner for success

Goal
Plan ahead to prevent challenging behaviors.

How
Identify elements that often lead to more challenging behaviors. Consider how set up the environment to reduce these triggers so the learner is more likely to succeed.

Context
Consider the context in which the learner typically engages in challenging behavior; then alter that environment to set the learner up for success.

Examples
- Change where the learner is sitting—minimize distraction
- Clear the table prior to starting homework to prevent throwing behavior
- Sit between learner and peer to prevent/block aggressive behavior

Tip
You can also alter the environment to promote positive behaviors.

Try
- Placing sensory items where the learner has easy access in order to promote appropriate sensory play
- Placing communication cards near the learner while they are working on a difficult task as a reminder of how to ask for help

At school

Alter the environment
By creating a clear workspace, the learner is more likely to attend to the task.

No alteration
When the workspace has items not necessary for the task, the learner is more likely to be distracted.

See visuals, pg. 141

In the community

1. Identify trigger

Recognize events or settings that may be a trigger for challenging behavior. For this learner, a peer approaching his toys is likely to lead to aggressive behavior.

2. Alter the environment

By intentionally changing the environment, the teacher is able to proactively plan for and prevent the challenging behavior. Here, the teacher sat close to the learner to encourage appropriate play with the peer.

2. No alteration

If no alteration is made, the challenging behavior is still likely to occur. Here, the teacher sat at a distance, and the learner was able to engage in aggressive behaviors when the peer approached him.

Priming

Preparing learners in advance to increase their chance of success

Goal

Increase the learner's success with an upcoming activity or event by preparing them for it in advance.

How

Prior to a situation that may be difficult for the learner, the teacher will inform the learner about what is upcoming.

This can be through the use of a time countdown ("Five minutes until bedtime") or a verbal reminder of expectations prior to a new situation ("We're going to a birthday party tomorrow; remember we will sit and watch Eva open her presents"). Priming can be used in the classroom by showing the learner the materials and modeling what to do prior to asking them to complete a new task.

Context

- Transitions
- Changes in schedule
- New situations
- Starting a task
- When preparing your learner for an upcoming event, remind them to use their coping skills if needed.

Tip

Try using a visual schedule to prime the learner for what will happen that day.

2

No prime, less success

By immediately presenting the difficult event (turning off electronics), learner may have little success with following through.

1

An upcoming event

Teacher will recognize that an upcoming event may be difficult for the learner.

See visuals, pg. 143

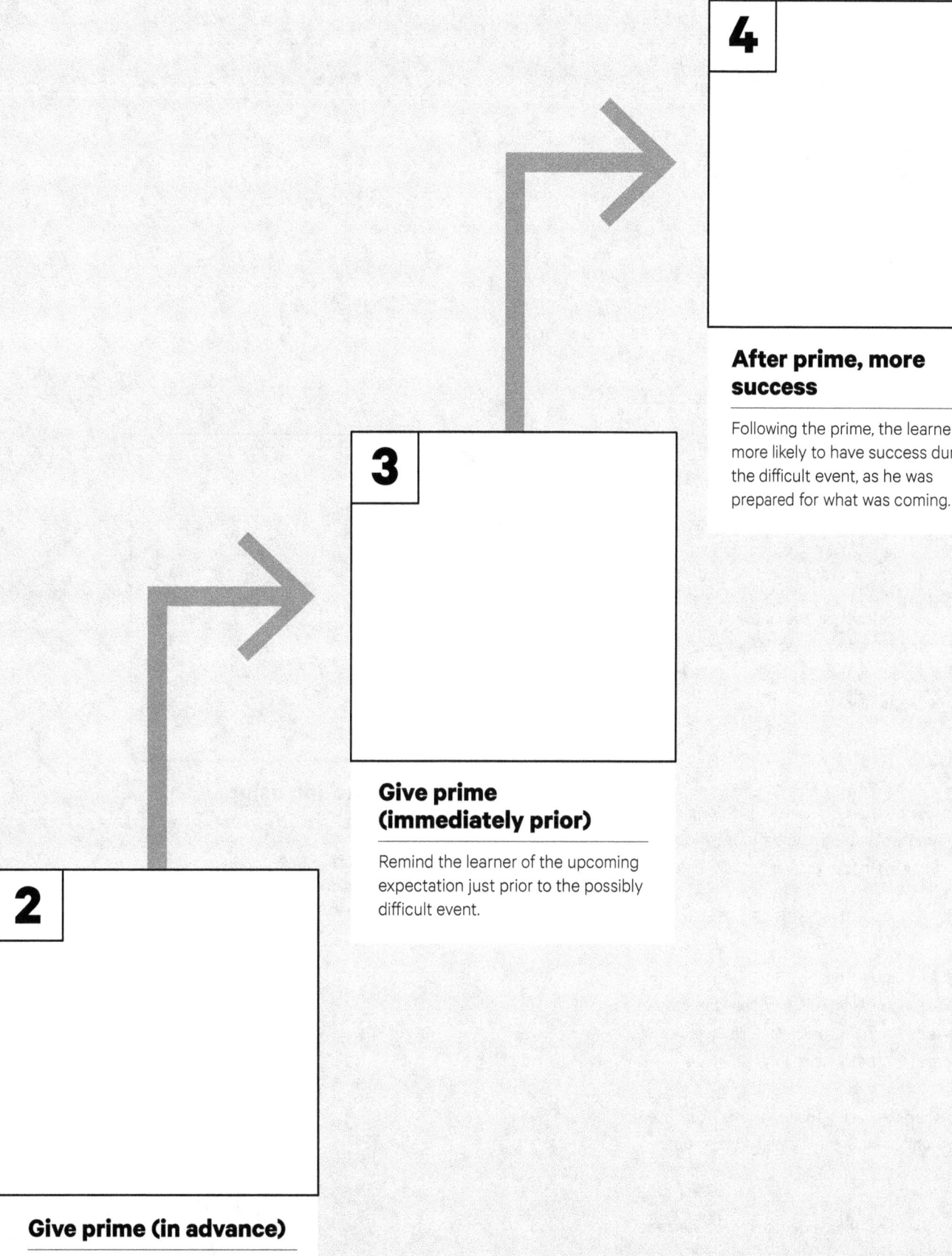

After prime, more success

Following the prime, the learner is more likely to have success during the difficult event, as he was prepared for what was coming.

Give prime (immediately prior)

Remind the learner of the upcoming expectation just prior to the possibly difficult event.

Give prime (in advance)

Give learner a prime in advance: either five minutes before a transition, or the day before a new event.

Official title: Premack Principle

First, Then

Using a simple statement to build motivation

Goal

Increase motivation in completing non-preferred tasks.

How

Identify a reward that will likely be motivating for the learner (e.g. time on electronics, favorite snack, tickles). Make a statement in the form: "first (target task), then (reward)." Only give the reward once the learner has completed the target task.

Context

This easy-to-use phrase can be inserted throughout the day in a variety of settings. Before giving a demand, think if you can re-word it using a "first, then" phrase.

Tip

Use specific and simple language. For example, instead of using words like "work hard," say the specific expectation (e.g. "finish five problems," "sit quietly at your desk," "read for ten minutes").

Use this tip when describing the reward, too (e.g. "five minutes with whiteboard," "sit in beanbag chair during story time").

Try using a visual "first, then" board to remind learners what they need to do in order to earn their reward.

1

Give instruction using "first, then"

State the target task followed by the reward that the learner will earn. Choose a reward that will likely be motivating to them.

See visuals, pg. 145

2

Follow through

Follow through with the demand by restating the "first, then" phrase until the learner has started doing the instruction. Remember to praise for starting the task!

3

Reinforcement

Following the completion of the task, remember to immediately provide the learner with the reward that was promised.

Official title: High probability, low probability sequence that creates behavior momentum

Easy, Easy, Hard

Creating momentum in starting a task

Goal

Learner will initiate a difficult target task (e.g. 'pick up your toys,' 'get on school bus,' 'complete ten math problems').

How

Increase the learner's motivation and engagement in starting a non-preferred task by starting with two back-to-back tasks that the learner is easily able to complete. Then, when you give the difficult task, the learner is already engaging in a pattern of following instructions. You are helping them get started; then by the time the difficult task is presented, they're already on a roll!

Context

This strategy can be used across different settings and for a wide variety of tasks. Consider which tasks are the hardest for your learner to get started (e.g. starting homework, cleaning up toys, starting bedtime routine, etc.). Then think of what easy instructions you could start with just prior to giving this tricky one!

Tip

When choosing easy tasks to give, make them related to the target task.

For example, if the target task is to start working on homework, first you could say "bring me backpack" (easy task), "sit down at table" (easy task). When you are ready to give the target task ("start your homework"), the learner has already started the task.

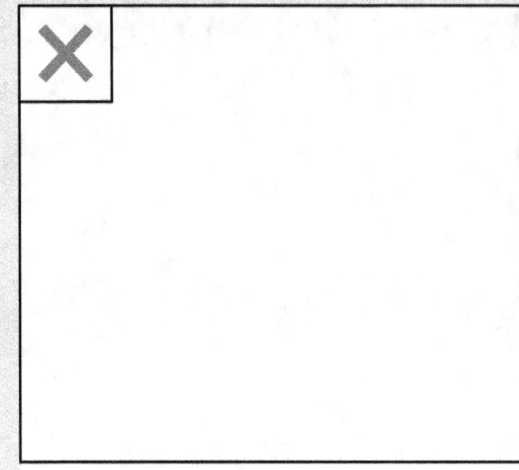

No initiation

By initially presenting a difficult task, the learner may feel overwhelmed, resulting in difficulty in initating the task.

First easy task

Start with a simple task that the learner can easily complete.

See visuals, pg. 147

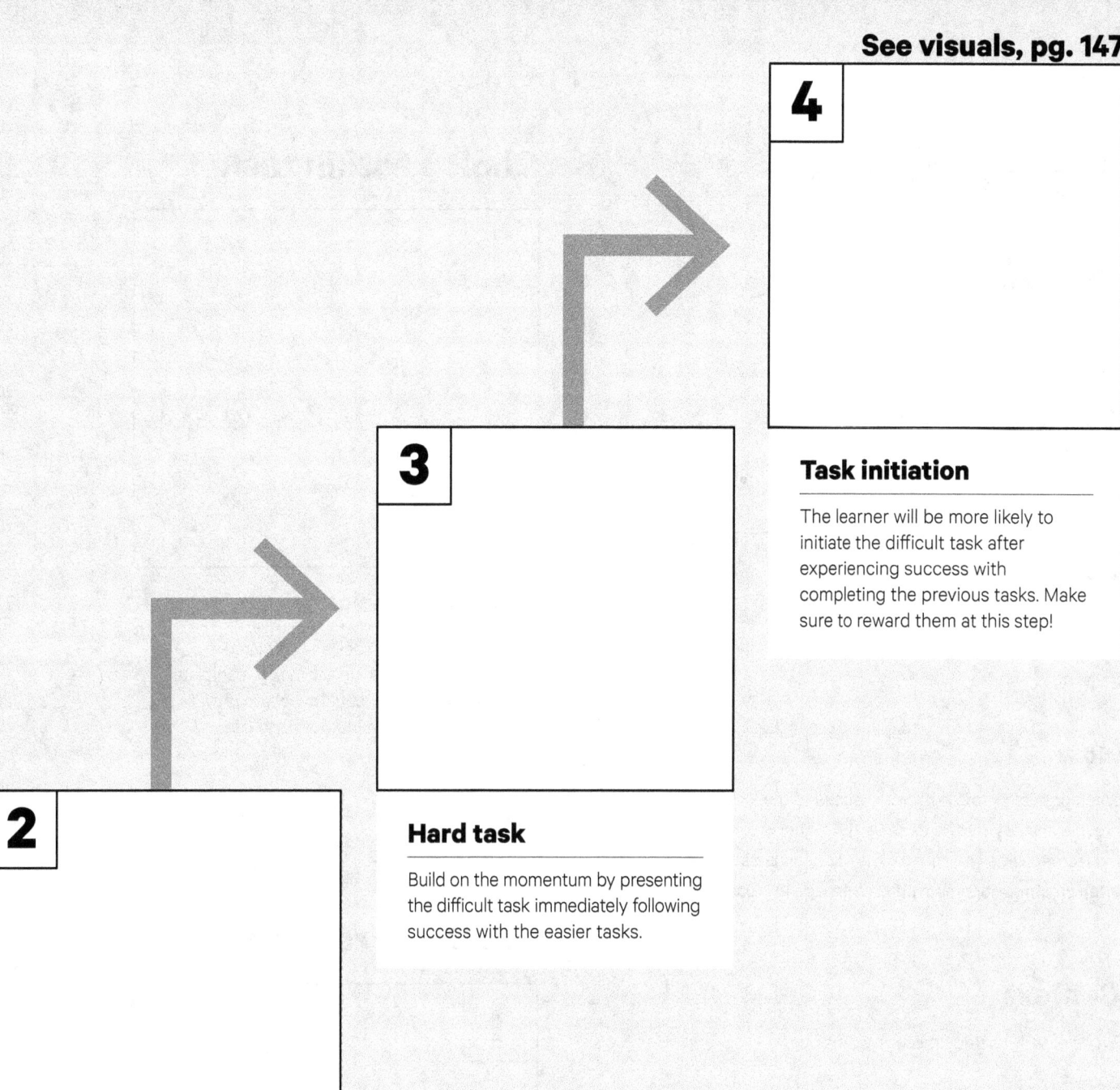

Task initiation

The learner will be more likely to initiate the difficult task after experiencing success with completing the previous tasks. Make sure to reward them at this step!

Hard task

Build on the momentum by presenting the difficult task immediately following success with the easier tasks.

Second easy task

Continue by immediately giving another easy task to complete.

Providing Choices

Offering shared control to increase motivation

Goal

By providing choices, the learner will be more likely to cooperate, be motivated to work, and stay engaged in the task.

How

When possible, provide choices related to the task and provide choices of rewards to earn. This helps give the learner some control over their daily expectations, often creating more motivation to engage in those expectations.

Context

Types of task-related choices may include:

- Order of tasks (e.g. reading or writing homework first)
- Materials to use (e.g. crayons or markers)
- Person to work with (e.g. Mom or Dad)
- Choosing where to sit (e.g. learner's desk or small table)

Tip

When offering choices for rewards, the teacher can ask, "Do you want to work for ____ or ____?"

For visual learners, the teacher may provide a visual of reward options from which the learner can choose.

Choice within task

1

→

Provide choice

The teacher provides a task-related choice: a choice of which task to complete first. The teacher could have also provided a choice of which toothpaste to use.

Choice of reward

1

→

Provide choice

Prior to giving the task demand (math test), the teacher provides choices of rewards that the learners can earn. This allows students to choose an individualized reward that will motivate them to work.

See visuals, pg. 149

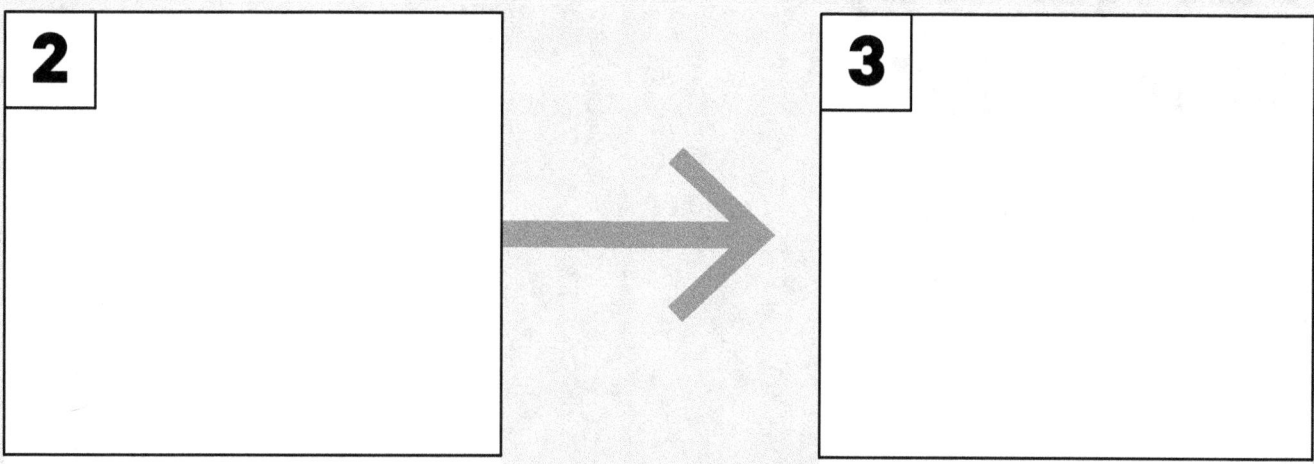

Learner makes choice

When the learner is given the opportunity to make their own choice, they have more control over the task which often leads to more cooperation.

Task completion

The learner is motivated to do the requested tasks in the order that they choose.

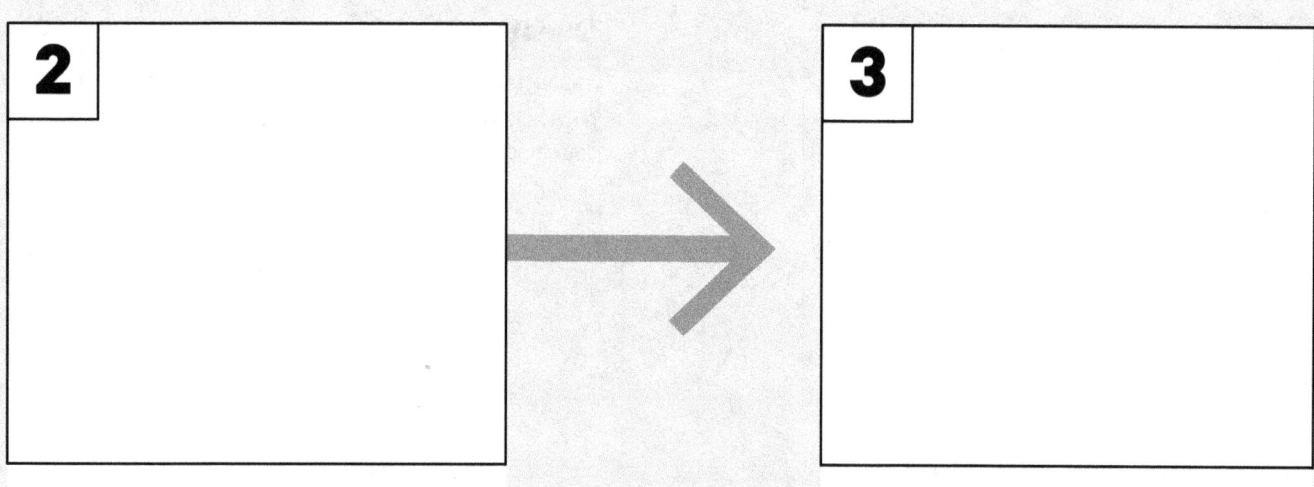

Learner makes choice

The learner has chosen a reward that is motivating for him. It may be helpful to keep this reward, or a picture of the reward, close by as a reminder for what he is working to earn.

Task completion

The learner is successful in completing the task and earns the reward he chose.

A Better Way to Say "No"

Two approaches to preventing challenging behaviors when the answer is "no"

Goal

Prevent challenging behaviors that typically arise when something is unavailable.

How

Hearing "no" or "wait" is difficult for many learners! Researchers evaluated different ways to say "no" or "wait" to determine which would result in the least challenging behaviors. They identified two successful approaches: "No + alternative" and "Yes, when…" Try switching up how you say "no" by using one of these sentence structures to respond! Interestingly, saying "no" + giving the rationale why something is unavailable at the moment was not successful at preventing challenging behaviors.

Context

Practice responding with one or both of these approaches if hearing "no" or "wait" is a common trigger for challenging behaviors for your learner.

Tip

To teach your learner to practice tolerating "no," you could set up a role play situation in which you tell the learner to make a request, but tell them in advance you're going to say "no." Instruct them to practice saying "ok" and choosing another activity to do. If they do this, immediately celebrate it by giving the item they initially requested. Over time, you can fade out the role plays and the big celebrations, but still remember to praise them, as this is a tricky skill across the ages!

Question

The learner asks for something that is not available right now or at all (the answer is "no" or "wait").

See visuals, pg. 151

2

No + alternative

When saying "no," provide two alternative options.

3

Accepts alternative

Research shows that when a learner is provided an alternative option, they are less likely to engage in challenging behaviors following the "no" response.

2

Yes, when...

If the learner can have what they are requesting, but just at a later time, respond with "yes, when... (when it is available)."

3

Waits

Research shows that when a learner is told "yes, when...," they are less likely to engage in the challenging behaviors that follow the "no" response.

Reactive Strategies

Official title: 3 Step Prompting

Tell, Show, Help

Three steps to consistently follow through

Note
These same three steps could also be used to teach a new skill! First, tell your learner how to do the skill, then model or role play the skill and then ask your learner to try on their own. If you add the fourth step of giving feedback, you are doing a highly effective teaching strategy called Behavior Skills Training (BST).

Goal
Improve consistency with follow-through when giving instructions and reduce the amount of repeated instructions.

How
When giving instructions that the learner has shown they can do, follow the three steps to gradually increase your support in assisting the learner with completing the instruction.

Tip
Place this visual strategy where the challenging target task usually occurs as a self-reminder for how to complete the steps (e.g. hang on learner's bedroom wall if 'get dressed' is a challenging task).

Context
Think about the instructions you find yourself repeating the most. That's when you should use this strategy!

Remember that when you give an instruction but don't follow through, the learner is learning it's ok to ignore that instruction. Be prepared to always follow through!

Tip
When giving an instruction, use a statement rather than asking the learner to complete the task.

Example
Don't say, "can you take off your shoes?" as the learner might respond, "no." Instead, say, "take off your shoes."

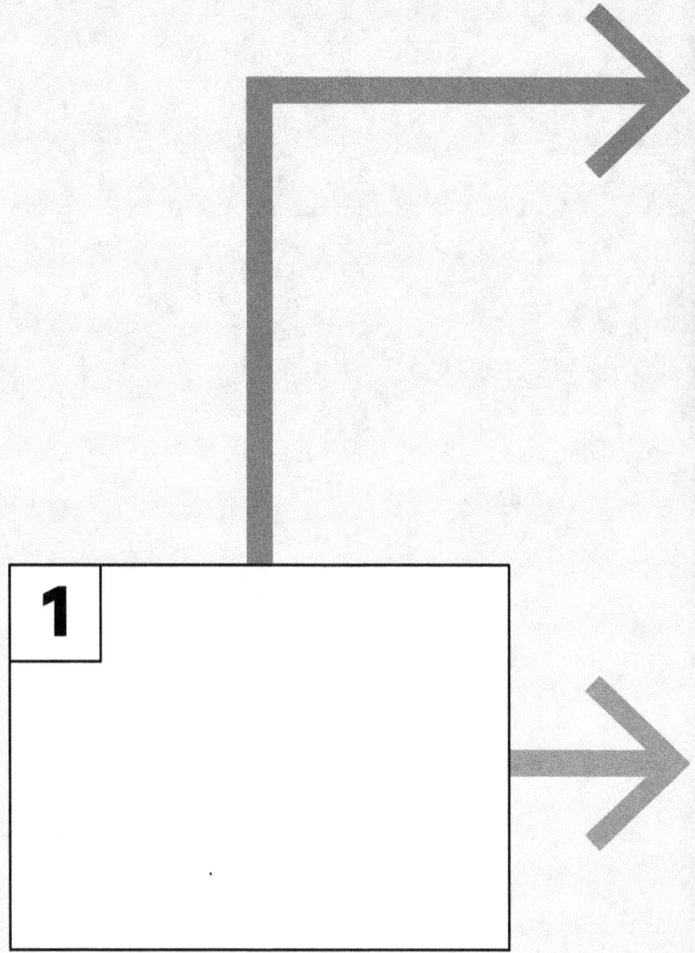

1

Tell
Give the verbal instruction and wait five seconds for the learner to start.

See visuals, pg. 153

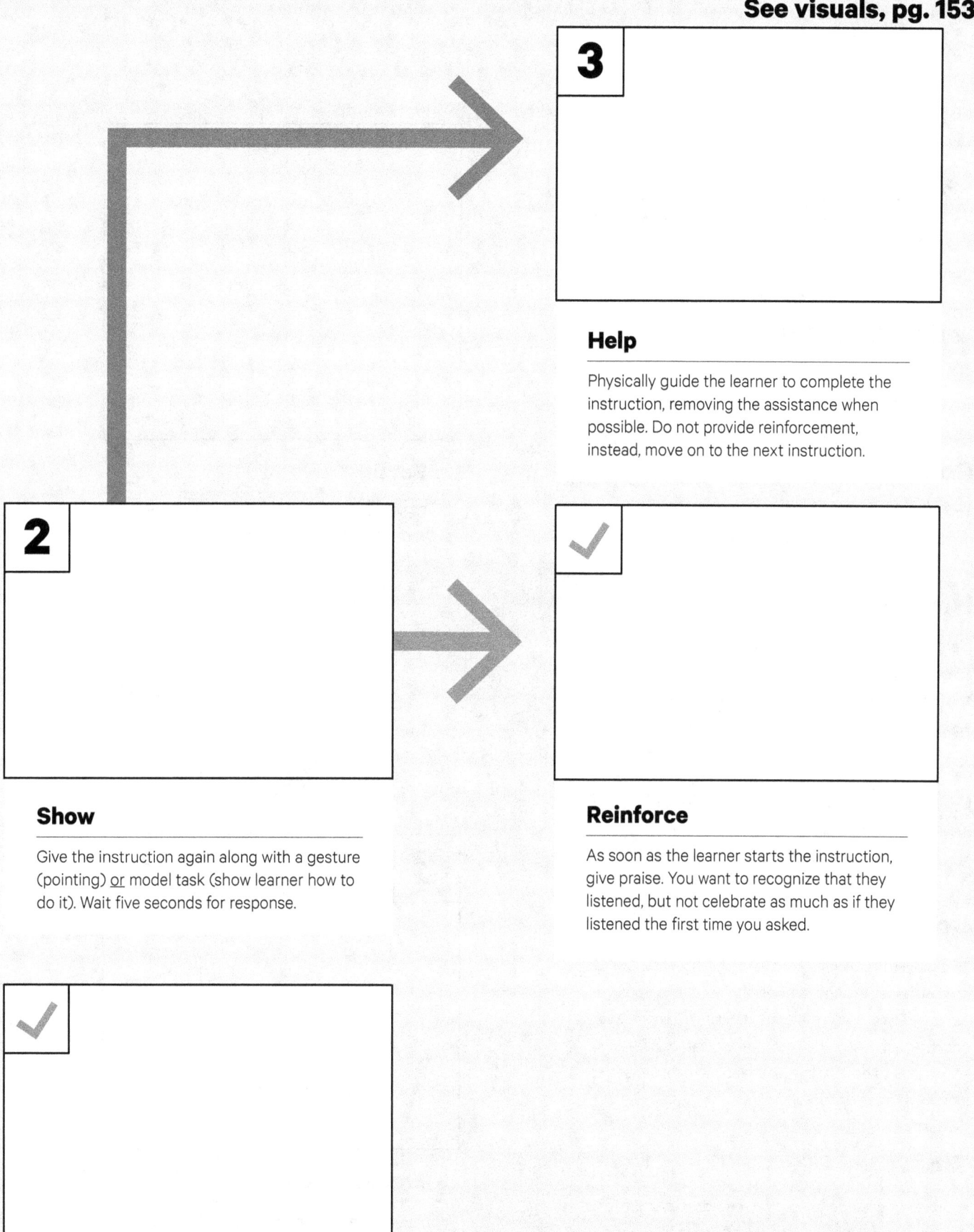

3

Help

Physically guide the learner to complete the instruction, removing the assistance when possible. Do not provide reinforcement, instead, move on to the next instruction.

2

Show

Give the instruction again along with a gesture (pointing) or model task (show learner how to do it). Wait five seconds for response.

Reinforce

As soon as the learner starts the instruction, give praise. You want to recognize that they listened, but not celebrate as much as if they listened the first time you asked.

Reinforce

As soon as the learner starts the instruction, give praise. Recognize and reward that they followed the instruction the first time you asked!

67

Official title: Token Economy

Token Boards

Creating clear expectations and clear rewards

Goal

Token boards help learners visualize progress towards a goal and learn to work for a delayed reward.

How

Identify 1 or 2 skills that you want to teach or promote. Then, determine what items or activities can be earned. Create rules for how tokens can be earned and when they can be exchanged for the reward. Make adjustments over time as needed such as increasing the number of tokens needed to earn the reward. Token boards should be used for more short-term teaching of new skills and then faded out to more natural ways of recognizing & celebrating progress.

Context

Token boards are commonly used in schools to reward on-task behaviors and families often use token boards (or "star charts") to reward independence in homework or chores. Choose behaviors that the learner already knows how to do but they just need more motivation to do it more often or consistently.

Tip

- Ask for the learner's input on rewards they'd like to earn. This will increase the motivation to work for them!
- Try making a customized token board with the learner's favorite characters as faces instead of stars.
- Make sure that the learner is earning the reward often enough for it to stay motivating.

Set up

Determine the rules for the token system and teach them to the learner.

3

Earning tokens

Add a token to the token board for each completed task or occurrence of a target behavior. When giving the token, make sure to say how they earned it to reinforce that behavior.

See visuals, pg. 155

1 Introduce

Remind the learner what task needs to be completed in order to earn a token, as well as what reward he is working to earn.

2 Provide praise

Provide praise when the learner completes the target task. Eventually, you will fade out the token board altogether and just keep the praise.

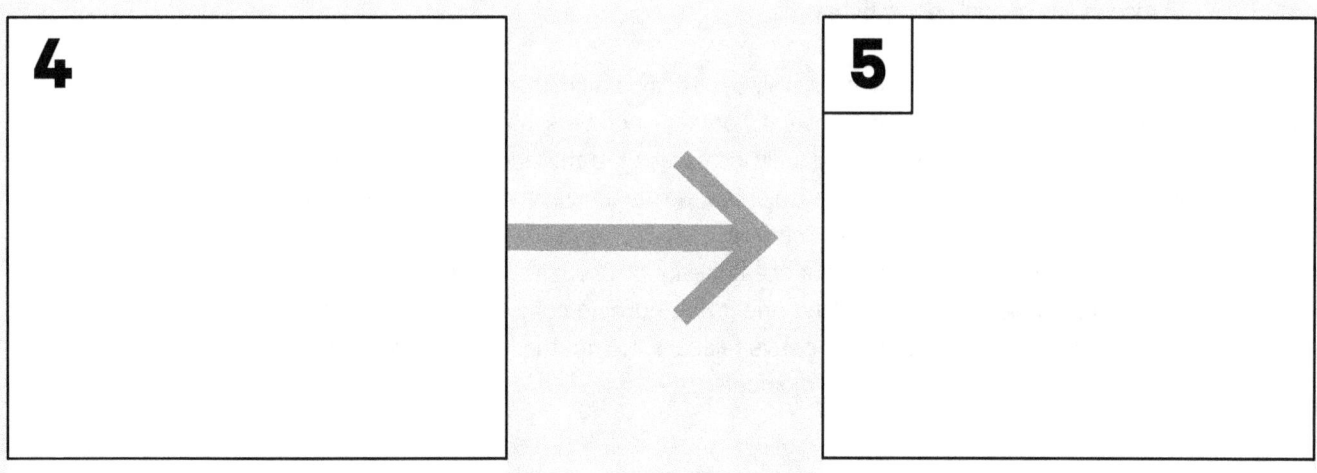

4 Earning rewards

Once the learner fills the token board with tokens, he earns the reward.

5 Reward

Give the reward as soon as the token board is full. The token board will be cleared and ready to use again.

A Note about Extinction

When aiming to reduce challenging behaviors, you may learn of an effective strategy called extinction. To give a brief introduction, extinction is when you identify why a learner is engaging in a challenging behavior and then don't allow the challenging behavior to obtain the same result anymore. Let's look at a common example: a child asks for candy at the check-out aisle of a store. The parent says "no," but then the child starts to cry loudly. The parent then gives the child the candy so they will stop crying. From this, we could say that the child maybe has learned that crying leads to them getting what they want (candy). In extinction, we want to un-teach this. So now, when the child cries because they want something, we won't give it to them. Extinction is when we stop responding in the way that has previously rewarded the challenging behavior. When using this strategy, it's important to know that an extinction burst may occur. An extinction burst simply means "it may get worse before it gets better." The learner is recognizing that what used to work (e.g. crying), isn't working anymore, so they might try increasing the amount or intensity of the behavior (e.g. crying longer, louder, or with more extreme behaviors like throwing or aggression). While this increase in challenging behaviors can seem worrisome, it's actually a sign that what you're doing is working, and it often only lasts for a very brief time. The best approach to utilizing extinction to support your learner is to use this strategy in combination with a skill-building strategy. We call this "Extinction + Redirection." Think of it like, "that's not how you get what you want, but here's how you can." See this visualized on page 76. While extinction is effective on its own, we recommend doing only the combination of Extinction + Redirection to the replacement behavior for the most ethical and compassionate approach to responding to challenging behaviors.

When used on its own, extinction is not always a compassionate approach to supporting our learners. If it's implemented inconsistently or team members "give in" during an extinction burst (when the behaviors have suddenly increased), the challenging behavior will become much more difficult to reduce. Because of this, we recommend only using extinction under the guidance of a BCBA or Behavior Specialist and not as a first line of intervention. Extinction can be a highly effective component of a behavior plan, but it's important to use it as just that—a component. We recommend prioritizing building communication skills, teaching self-advocacy, and maintaining a positive relationship with the learner by supporting and validating them during challenging moments.

Extinction by Function

Access and attention

Goal

Change the way we respond to challenging behaviors.

How

First, we need to understand why a challenging behavior is happening in order to stop reinforcing that behavior (encouraging it to continue happening). To do this, collect ABC data to determine the function. Once we understand what is reinforcing the behavior (the function), we can use extinction to stop responding in that way.

Context

Use this strategy with the guidance of an ABA professional. They can assist in determining the function and guiding the most ethical implementation. Extinction can be very effective at reducing challenging behaviors, but be sure you are doing it correctly and compassionately.

Tip

There is a misconception that extinction always means we are ignoring the learner. We never want to ignore a person, especially someone in distress. If you believe the behavior is attention-seeking, you can reduce the attention you give to the behavior, not the person.

Here's how: keep your face neutral, avoid eye contact, and refrain from giving reprimands.

Challenging behavior

This visual illustrates how a challenging behavior could be occurring for any of the four functions and how extinction would look different for each one.

Note

See Extinction + Redirection to learn how to turn tricky moments into teaching moments to most effectively and ethically support your learner.

See visuals, pg. 157

Function **access**

1 → **2**

Learned behavior

They have learned through experience that engaging in the behavior leads to accessing a preferred item.

Here, Kate has learned that she can play with her favorite bunny when asked to put away the crayons she threw.

Use extinction

Following the behavior, don't provide access to preferred items.

Here, another student is putting away the thrown crayons which prevents Kate from getting to play with the bunny.

Function **attention**
(planned ignoring)

1 → **2**

Learned behavior

They have learned through experience that engaging in the behavior leads to getting attention from others.

Here, Kate has learned that when she throws crayons, her teacher reprimands her, and maybe she thinks that's funny.

Use extinction

Refrain from giving unnecessary attention to the behavior (e.g. reactions, reprimands). Remain calm and neutral.

Here, the teacher is not responding to Kate's throwing behavior, as it's not harming anyone.

73

Extinction by Function

Escape and sensory

Goal

Change the way we respond to challenging behaviors.

How

First, we need to understand why a challenging behavior is happening in order to stop reinforcing that behavior (encouraging it to continue happening). To do this, collect ABC data to determine the function. Once we understand what is reinforcing the behavior (the function), we can use extinction to stop responding in that way.

Context

Use this strategy with the guidance of an ABA professional. They can assist in determining the function and guiding the most ethical implementation. Extinction can be very effective at reducing challenging behaviors, but be sure you are doing it correctly and compassionately.

Tip

When the function is escape, try using the Tell, Show, Help strategy to consistently follow through in a supportive way.

In sensory extinction, you are attempting to block the learner from receiving the sensory input. We do not recommend physically blocking someone, especially from engaging in a behavior they could be using to self-soothe. Here, we've illustrated how to alter the environment to block sensory input.

Challenging behavior

This visual illustrates how a challenging behavior could be occurring for any of the four functions and how extinction would look different for each one.

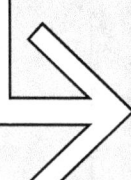

See visuals, pg. 159

Function **escape**

1 **Learned behavior**

They have learned through experience that engaging in the behavior leads to escaping a non-preferred task.

Here, Kate has learned that if she throws crayons, she can get out of some of the work by being sent to the rug.

2 **Use extinction**

Following the behavior, continue to follow through with the initial instruction to avoid them escaping or delaying the task.

Here, the teacher is giving a reminder of the expectation.

Function **sensory**

1 **Learned behavior**

They have learned through experience that engaging in the behavior leads to an enjoyable feeling or helps with self-regulation.

Here, Kate has found that crayons make a cool noise when they hit the ground. While fun, it's distracting her from her work.

2 **Use extinction**

If the sensory behavior is causing harm to self or others or is disruptive to learning, identify ways that you can alter the environment to limit the sensory sensation.

Here, the teacher has placed a rug so the crayons don't make a noise when they hit the ground.

Extinction + Redirection

Responding with support

Goal

Turn a tricky moment into a teaching moment by redirecting to a better behavior.

How

First, determine why the target challenging behavior is occurring (the function). Then, when the behavior occurs, change your typical response from enabling that function to redirecting to a better behavior. The better behavior should match the function, meaning you are redirecting them to a better way to get their needs met.

Context

We've illustrated what this strategy would look like across each function. Refer back to the previous pages so you can see the difference between just using extinction to reduce a challenging behavior versus here, adding in redirection to actually support the learner with what they need.

Note

In each of these scenarios, the learner has started with a challenging behavior, and the teacher has reminded them of a better way to communicate their needs. It's important to note that if they respond to this redirection, we want to celebrate it, but not as much as if they had done this behavior independently. For example, if they ask for a break after you gave that reminder, maybe only give a 1 minute break instead of a 5 minute break. We want them to recognize that it's better to do the better behavior independently the first time (in ABA jargon, this is called "matching law").

Sensory

When a learner is engaging in a behavior for sensory input, it's difficult for us to prevent this sensation without physically stopping them, which is not recommended. Instead, remind them they can ask for a sensory break, sensory item, or support with using a coping strategy.

Remember that just because an individual is engaging in a sensory behavior, it does not necessarily make it a "challenging behavior" that we need to redirect. Look out for behaviors that are causing harm to self or others or are impeding their learning.

See visuals, pg. 161

Attention

Continue to remain neutral, but now also add in a reminder of how they can better gain your attention or the attention of others.

It's helpful if this reminder is done through visuals or modeling, where you are limiting how much you are verbally instructing them. Here, the teacher is modeling raising his hand as a reminder of that expectation.

Access

Continue to withhold the item or activity the learner was attempting to get by engaging in the challenging behavior, but now also add in a reminder of how they can better ask for what they want.

This reminder can be a verbal reminder, as seen in this illustration, or it could be a visual that you provide or point to. For AAC users, point to the symbol on their core board or device as a way to remind them how to better request.

Escape

Continue to follow through with the given instruction or expectation (see Tell, Show, Help strategy), but now also add in a reminder of how they can better ask for help or a break if needed.

It might help here to remind your learner of what they are working toward as a way to build motivation in the moment.

Official title: Response blocking + redirection

Blocking Unsafe Behaviors

A three-step approach to responding to unsafe behaviors

Goal
Have a calm, consistent response to unsafe behaviors.

How
When a learner attempts an unsafe behavior, the teacher will first block the behavior, then immediately redirect the learner to the appropriate behavior (the replacement skill).

It is important that the teacher first understands why the unsafe behavior is occurring (the function), so they can redirect to an effective replacement behavior.

Context
Use this strategy following learner engagement or attempt at an unsafe behavior such as aggression, elopement (running away), or self-injurious behaviors.

Blocking is actually a punishment procedure, as it aims to reduce the behavior that just occurred. Make sure that if you use this strategy, your behavior plan also includes (and prioritizes) a reinforcement strategy.

Tip
Educators and service providers should not be placing their hands on a learner unless they are trained in safe crisis management (i.e. CPI certified). If your learner often engages in unsafe behaviors, collaborate with the team to create a Behavior Escalation Plan.

1

Unsafe behavior
The learner approaches the teacher and attempts an unsafe behavior.

Note: The teacher is already aware why this learner engages in hitting. Here, the function is to get attention.

See visuals, pg. 163

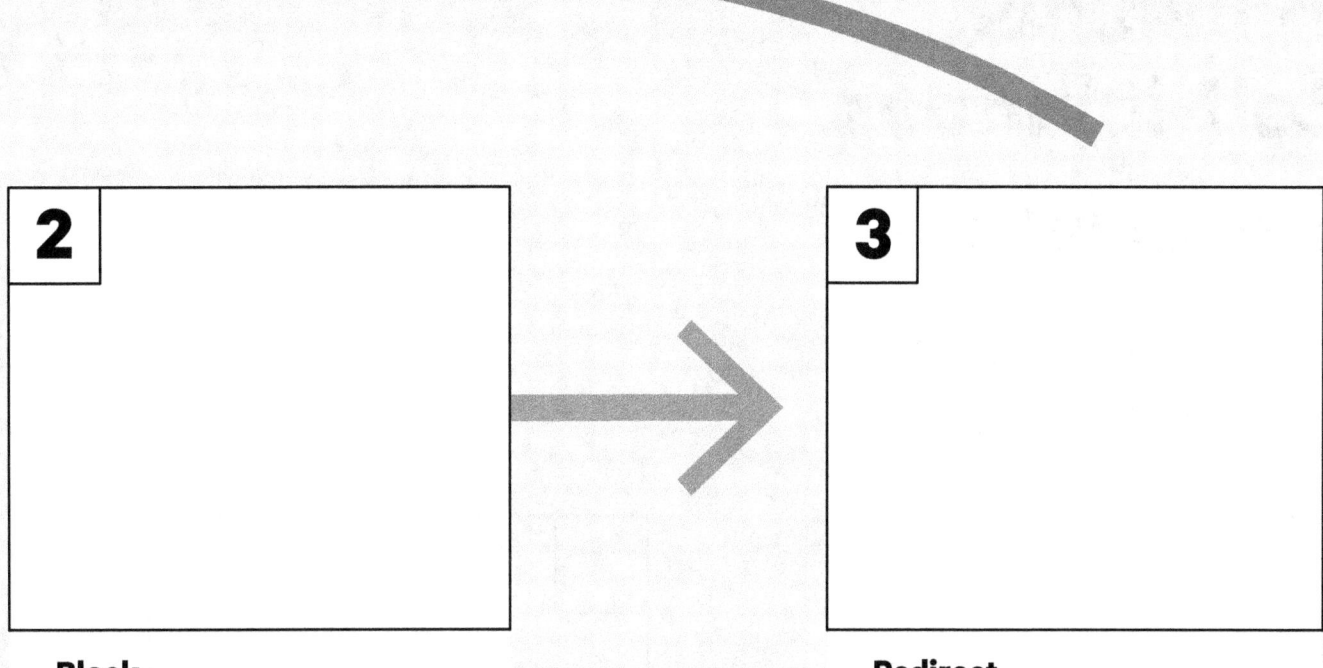

Block

The teacher blocks the unsafe behavior.

Redirect

The teacher redirects the learner to a more appropriate behavior.

Here, the teacher is modeling how to tap on her shoulder in order to get attention. The teacher is turned away from the learner (not giving attention), until the learner does the better behavior (tapping on the shoulder).

Reinforce appropriate behavior

Once the learner has engaged in the appropriate behavior, the teacher will provide reinforcement.

Here, the learner is tapping on the teacher's shoulder to request attention. This is appropriate, so the teacher turns and gives attention.

Note

Whenever a learner is given a chance to try again and then engages in the appropriate behavior, we want to celebrate this, but not as much as if they had engaged in the appropriate behavior independently to begin with. We want to recognize progess, but really celebrate independence!

Official title: Response Interruption and Redirection

Managing Self-injurious Behaviors

A gentle response to repetitive, self-injurious behaviors

Goal

In the moment, decrease self-injurious behaviors by redirecting to another behavior.

How

When a self-injurious behavior occurs, immediately interrupt the behavior and redirect the learner to another behavior. If you know the function of the behavior, redirect to another behavior that meets that same need. If you don't know the function yet, redirect to another behavior that will keep the learner safe in that moment.

Context

Use this strategy to respond to repetitive self-injurious behaviors such as head banging, self-biting, picking at skin, or mouthing inedible objects. This strategy is actually a punishment strategy that has shown to be effective at reducing behaviors that are based in sensory needs.

Tip

When choosing a replacement behavior for a sensory need, it's important to understand what about the self-injurious behavior is soothing to them. For example, in head banging, do they like the head movement feeling or is it the pressure of the contact with a hard surface? The more specific you can understand the need, the more effective your replacement behavior will be.

Self-injurious behavior

A self-injurious behavior occurs.

Here, the learner is head-banging against the wall after coloring outside of the lines on his drawing.

See visuals, pg. 165

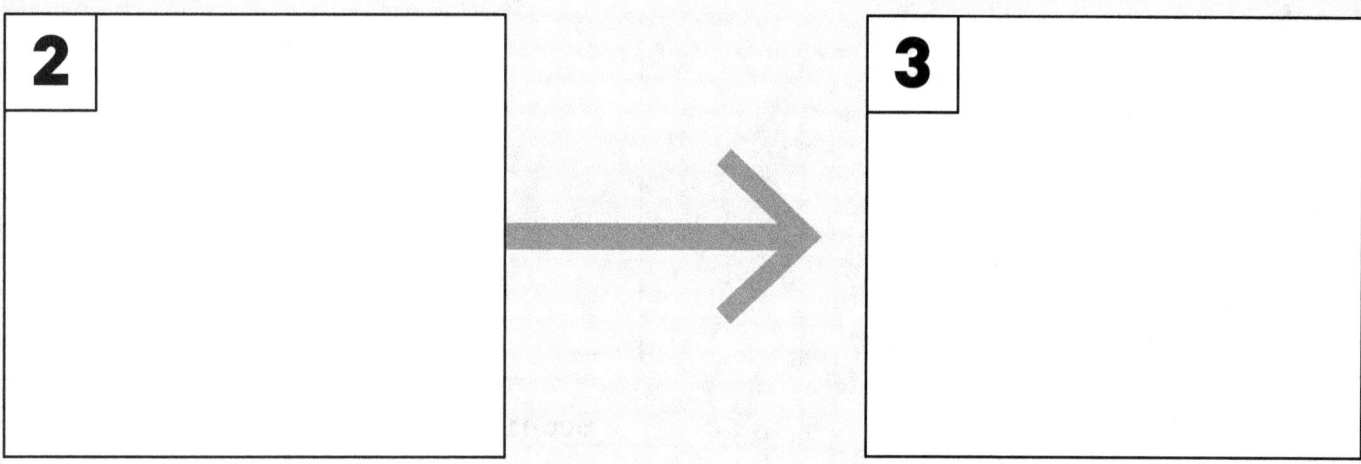

Interrupt

Interrupt, or block, the behavior. Use as little physical contact as possible.

Educators and service providers should have proper training if utilizing hands-on methods.

Redirect

Redirect the learner to engage in a behavior that cannot be done at the same time as the self-injurious behavior. Try redirecting to a coping skill like taking deep breaths.

Official title: Differential Reinforcement

3 Reward Options

Three approaches to improving one behavior

Goal

Provide clarity in the differences between these commonly used, yet misunderstood, reward strategies.

How

First, identify the target challenging behavior and its function. Then, determine the team's priority goal: building communication, teaching tolerance, or maintaining safety. Deciding which goal takes precedence guides the decision of which reward option to choose.

Context

An ABA provider or Behavior Specialist will be able to help determine which reward option is right for you and your learner. Once a decision is made, this strategy will be part of the team's behavior plan that everyone will implement.

Tip

You can always start with one; then once your goal is met, move to another! For example, if the learner has limited communication skills, start with DRA. Once they've learned to consistently communicate their wants and needs, you could move to DRI where they learn to tolerate when what they requested is not available. Another example is if your learner is engaging in high rates of dangerous behaviors at school, although they have strong communication skills. We would first start with a DRO to aim to reduce that behavior from happening, and then move to a DRI to target their engagement in academic activities.

Scenario

In this example scenario, the learner struggles with sharing and often grabs items from others, occasionally also hitting or pinching them (function: access).

Determine the team's priority goal: building communication, teaching tolerance, or maintaining safety. Based on this, choose one of the reward strategies to include in your behavior plan for the entire team to consistently implement.

No matter which reward option you choose, initially, we want to reward every success. Over time, you can fade out this reward, but at the beginning, consistent rewards will lead to faster progress!

See visuals, pg. 167

DRA option: Building communication

In Differential Reinforcement of an Alternative Behavior (DRA), we are aiming to build a behavior that is a better way for them to access or express their wants and needs. This behavior matches the function of the challenging behavior, meaning it's just a better way for them to get what they want or need. In a DRA, we are often recognizing their engagement in communication skills like asking for help, a break, space, more time, items/activities, or attention by rewarding them with exactly what they asked for.

DRI option: Teaching tolerance

In Differential Reinforcement of an Incompatible Behavior (DRI), we are aiming to build a behavior of a specific expectation. This often involves tolerating something they may not particularly want to do, but need to do, including going to school, taking turns, completing assignments, keeping hands to self, and following directions. The team will choose one specific behavior to build and then determine a reward that the learner can earn for engaging in this expected behavior.

DRO option: Maintaining safety

In Differential Reinforcement of Other Behavior (DRO), our focus is on reducing the challenging behavior by rewarding times that it did not occur. They do not have to engage in any specific behavior to earn the reward. First, determine how often the behavior is occurring and then create a schedule where the learner can earn a reward for going a specific amount of time (just less than their baseline) without engaging in the target challenging behavior. In this example, the learner was grabbing items and hitting his sister about every 20 minutes. The mom set up a schedule where every 15 minutes that he goes without grabbing/hitting, he earns a reward.

Teaching New Skills

> Official title: Pairing

Rapport Building

Establishing a connection as the foundation of learning

Goal

Set the tone for learning by creating and maintaining a genuine positive relationship.

How

Before teaching any new skills, it's essential that a trusting relationship is formed. A leader in the ABA field, Greg Hanley, says that individuals learn best when they are "happy, relaxed, and engaged." To establish this, spend time just playing with the learner and getting to know them! Be engaged in their favorite items and activities without giving any demands or asking questions. Just have fun! Then, when you introduce a new skill or new person, because you have built a foundation of trust, they will likely be more open to it.

Context

Building and maintaining rapport ('Pairing') should always be happening, but it's especially important when establishing a new relationship like with a new teacher, interventionist, or friend. With ABA clients, ensure that the first few sessions are filled with pairing. Then continue to make time for pairing on an ongoing basis. Parents & teachers can benefit from pairing too! Much of their role involves giving instructions. We recommend a goal of playing for 5 minutes per day with no demands or questions.

Tip

Try saving special toys or activities that you two only do together. Pairing is all about building and sustaining a genuine connection!

Pair yourself

1

Identifying preferences

Get to know your learner! Find out what their favorite items/activities are.

Pair peers

1

Identifying preferences

Get to know your learner! Find out what their favorite items/activities are.

Official title: Natural Environment Teaching (NET)

Personalized Teaching

Creating teaching moments within a typical day

Goal

Blend teaching into common and preferred activities.

How

Consider the typical activities that the learner engages in and what their preferences are. Now, review the skills that you've identified to teach the learner. Use your creativity to think about how you can teach those skills during these common and preferred activities.

For example, a common ABA goal is teaching a learner to ask for help. You could create opportunities to practice this skill in their typical day by putting the toothbrush/toothpaste out of reach in the morning, then putting the snack inside a hard-to-open container and then doing an art project that requires some assistance.

Context

You can use this approach to teach any skill! It just takes some planning and creativity to determine how to blend teaching moments into typical daily activities. The more that you can teach skills during play, the less you'll need to do a "work then play" structure. This teaching method also works well for teaching social skills, community skills, independence skills, and safety skills, as these are helpful to practice in real-life scenarios.

Tip

Follow their lead! Pay attention to what they enjoy doing and think, "How can I turn this into a learning moment?"

1

Identify

Get to know your learner! Learn all about their preferences and typical daily activities. Then (with the guidance of an ABA provider), choose a target skill to teach.

2

Instruction

Blend teaching the target new skill into the learner's preferred or typical activities.

Here, the team has chosen following one-step instructions as the target skill for this learner. We recommend having 3 different 'targets' or instructions for each skill (e.g. "Put ___," "Stir," "Show ____") so they can learn to differentiate.

See visuals, pg. 169

2

Play with no demands

Join in on their favorite activity and play without giving any demands (including 'play demands' like "push it this way" or "go faster"). Follow their lead! You want to prioritize comments over questions during this time (e.g. "It's so fast!" instead of "Where is it going?").

Note

This strategy is a great choice for a staff or parent training goal! Set the expectation that they will engage in demand-free, child-led play for 5 minutes per session or per day.

2

Assist in pairing peer

Set up an opportunity to build a positive relationship with a peer by finding an activity they both enjoy and helping the peer join in.

3

Assist in peer play

By giving opportunities for peers to just play together without further expectations, they can develop their shared interests and build their social connection!

87

See visuals, pg. 171

Incorrect

Even though the instruction was given during play, we are still targeting teaching this skill, so if the learner does not follow the instruction, give them feedback and reset to try again.

Try again

Give the initial instruction again, but this time you might need to add an additional 'prompt,' or hint, like pointing at what they should do or modeling the action for them. If they follow the instruction this time, recognize it, but not as excitedly as if they did it independently the first time.

Correct

If the learner follows the instruction the first time asked, celebrate! As we are teaching a new skill, it's helpful to give "behavior-specific praise," meaning, say exactly what they did well.

Reward

In naturalistic teaching, the reward is built into the play or activity! For example, a natural reward for paying at a restaurant is getting your food, whereas a reward for putting on your shoes could be going to the park. Here, the teacher is continuing to play pretend kitchen with the learner.

Official title: Functional Communication Training + Differential Reinforcement

Building Better Behaviors

Replacing a challenging behavior with a better behavior

Goal

Reduce challenging behaviors by teaching a more appropriate, alternative behavior.

How

Identify why a challenging behavior is occurring, and then teach the learner a better, more appropriate, way to get their needs met. Only reinforce this better behavior, and if the challenging behavior occurs, remind them what they should do instead.

Context

In a recent research study with over 100 children with developmental delays and destructive behaviors, just teaching a better behavior led to a 90% reduction in their challenging behaviors. This is the most impactful skill you can teach! Teaching this new, better behavior should happen when learners are happy, relaxed, and engaged. Better behaviors often include "functional communication," meaning better ways to request wants/needs. This may include asking for help, a break, more time, space, clarification, expressions of self-advocacy, to be included in a social activity, etc.

Tip

It's essential that you consider how your learner learns best. Try using visuals, modeling, role play, or nearby peers to help teach this better behavior. Create many opportunities to teach and practice this skill, both at home and at school.

1

Identify the target and the function of behavior

Here, the learner is calling out to get the teacher's attention. First, identify the specific behavior you want to reduce. Then, use the ABC Chart to determine the function.

2

Teach a replacement behavior

Teach the learner a better way to express their needs. There are many ways to teach a new behavior. You can explain it, model it, or use visuals!

Here, the teacher is proactively showing the learner that if he wants the teacher's attention, he should raise his hand instead of yelling out.

See visuals, pg. 173

4

Amount of reinforcement

The more independently the learner is engaging in the better behavior, the more reinforcement he should receive. Here the teacher is providing extra attention by coming to the learner's desk to call on him.

3

&

Reinforce the better behavior

Every time the learner engages in the better behavior, immediately give reinforcement (here, the teacher is providing attention by calling on the learner). If the learner engages in challenging behavior, move back to step 2. Remind them of what behavior they should do.

Reinforce others

Provide reinforcement (here, giving attention) to other nearby learners who are engaging in the better behavior. This will give a hint to the learner of what he should do to get what he wants (here, attention).

Official title: Total task chaining using a task analysis

Breaking Down Skills

Teaching a new, complex skill

Goal

Teach a new, complex skill by breaking it down into a sequence of smaller step.

How

The teacher will develop the task analysis (TA) by writing down the small steps necessary to complete the task/activity.

The teacher will systematically teach each step, one at a time, providing assistance as needed. Over time, the prompts (assistance) are faded out, resulting in the learner becoming independent in this skill!

Context

Task analyses are often used to teach adaptive skills such as washing hands, brushing teeth, getting dressed, tying shoes, doing chores, making a meal, and crossing the street. Create a task analysis for any complex skill that can be broken down into simple steps.

Tip

Remember to practice the steps yourself after you have created the TA to ensure that they are in correct sequence and nothing was left out. Often, visuals are a great way to assist in learning the skill sequence
Try to reduce teacher assistance and increase learner independence each time the skill is practiced.

1

Write the steps

Teacher will write down the steps needed to complete the task. Each step should be one simple action.

4

Assist learner through steps: model

Another way to provide assistance with a step is through a model prompt, where you show the learner how to do the step by first doing it yourself.

See visuals, pg. 175

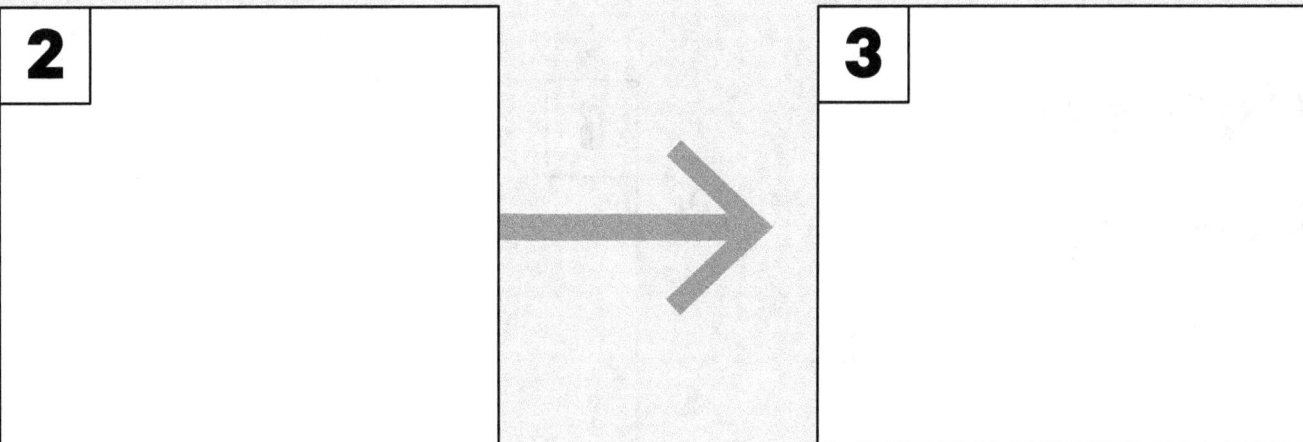

2

Assist learner through steps: gesture

If the learner needs assistance, provide a prompt, or reminder of what to do. One way to do that is through gesturing, or pointing. This father is pointing to the faucet to remind the learner to turn on water.

3

Assist learner through steps: vocal

Another way to provide assistance with a step is using a vocal prompt, or telling the learner what to do. Try to limit using this type of prompt, as it can be harder to fade out (the learner can become more dependent on them).

5

Reinforce independence

For any step that the learner does independently, provide praise (and refrain from prompting).

6

Reinforce learning

Provide specific praise (stating exactly what was done well) anytime the learner completes a step indepedently for the first time.

Problem-Solving

Teaching independence in finding solutions

Goal

Improve independent problem-solving skills across a variety of situations.

How

Guide the learner through each step in the problem-solving process while emphasizing their collaboration and eventual independence.

Context

Use these steps each time a new problem arises. The process is the same whether it is a small problem (e.g. running out of notebook paper) or a bigger problem (e.g. being bullied at school).

Tip

When the learner provides a solution suggestion (no matter how silly!), always play it out (in real life or via conversation), so they can learn on their own to determine if it was an effective solution or not.

1

Problem
Learner encounters a problem.

4

Choose
Encourage the learner to choose one solution and try it.

See visuals, pg. 177

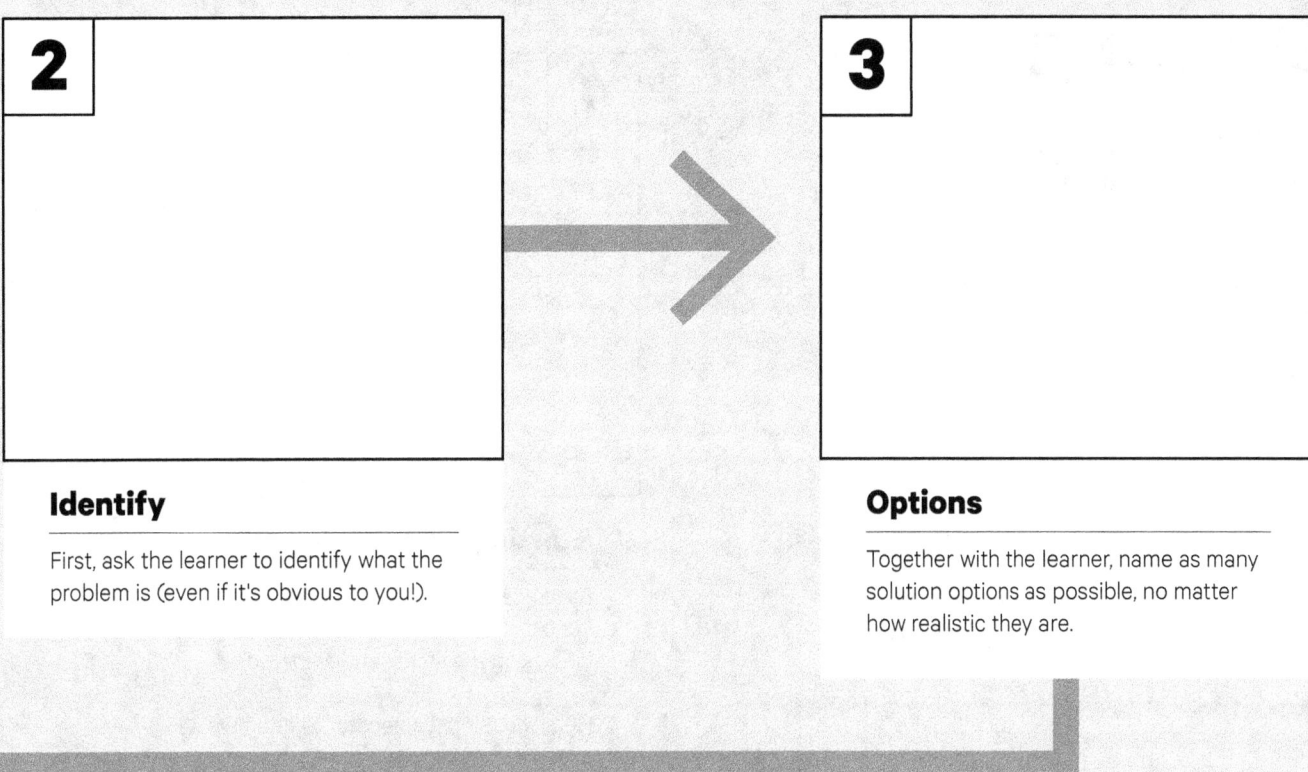

2

Identify

First, ask the learner to identify what the problem is (even if it's obvious to you!).

3

Options

Together with the learner, name as many solution options as possible, no matter how realistic they are.

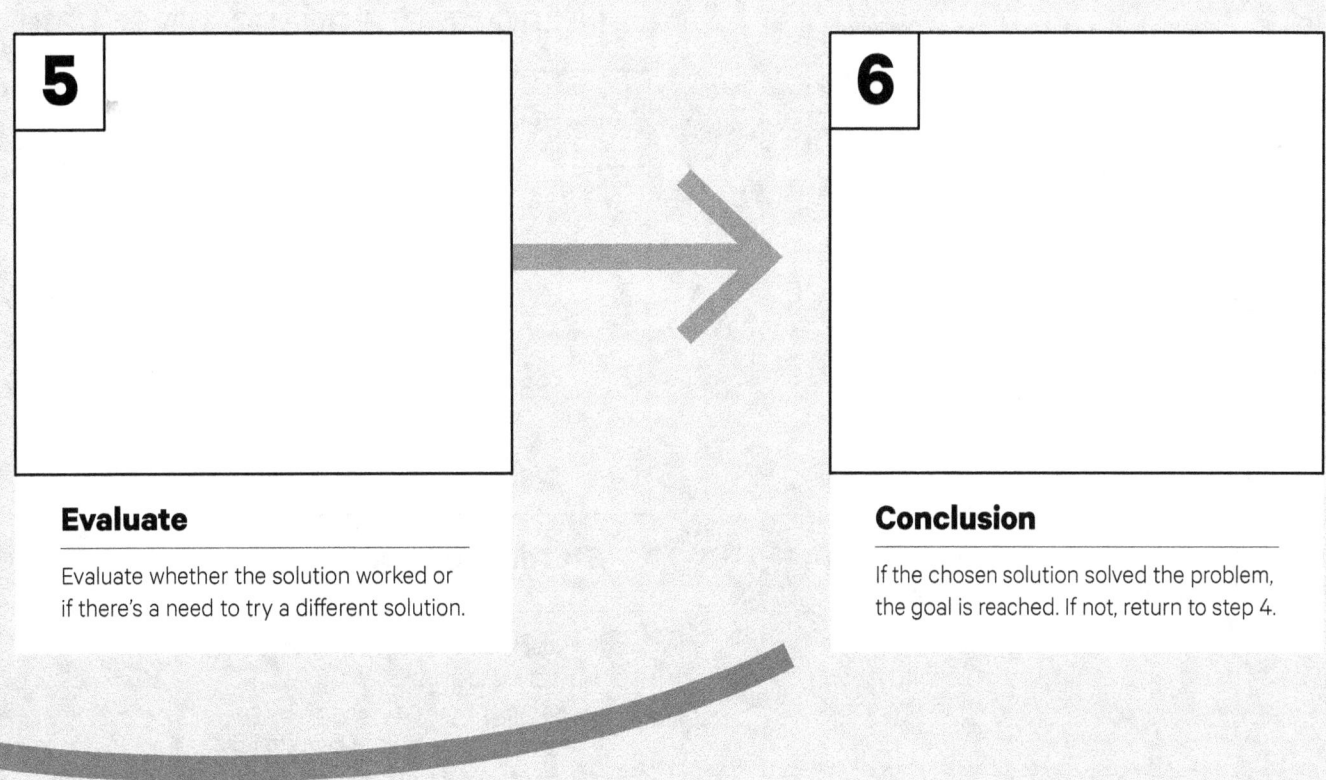

5

Evaluate

Evaluate whether the solution worked or if there's a need to try a different solution.

6

Conclusion

If the chosen solution solved the problem, the goal is reached. If not, return to step 4.

95

Shaping & Fading

Teaching a new skill over time

Goal

Shaping & Fading are often confused because they both aim to teach a new skill over time. Shaping aims to gradually build a new skill over time, where with fading, the learner is becoming more independent with a skill over time.

How

Reinforce the learner's progress in coming closer and closer to the actual target skill. This can be done over time (as in the first visual example) or during one sitting with repeated tries (as in the second visual example).

To shape a skill, start by teaching a small part of the skill and continue to build the skill with practice.
In fading, start by providing full support and then fade out your assistance over time.

Context

Shaping is frequently used when teaching language, tolerance, and attending skills. You could first teach your learner to attend to independent work for 30 seconds, then 1 minute, then 2 minutes.

Fading is often used when teaching adaptive skills, starting with full teacher assistance and then gradually letting the learner become more independent.

Shaping
Building a skill over time

Starting to learn

Reinforce any initiation in a new skill. For expressive communication, this could be making the first sound of the word.

Here, the reinforcement for all attempts of saying "cookie" will be giving the cookie to the learner.

Fading
Building independence over time

Starting to learn

Reinforce any initiation in a new skill. For adaptive skills, you may need to start with full assistance. Here, the reinforcement can be giving praise, or giving access to a favorite item after the learner has practiced the new skill.

See visuals, pg. 179

2

Improving

Reinforce progress. Once the learner has improved on the skill, only reinforce that level of the skill (e.g. do not give a cookie if he only says "kuh").

Note that the teacher is always saying the full, correct word ("cookie") when giving it as a reward.

3

Independent

Once the learner has mastered the skill, only reinforce that level of the skill (e.g. only give the cookie if he says "cookie").

2

Improving

Reinforce progress. As the learner is improving, slowly remove your assistance, which will increase their independence.

3

Independent

Fade your assistance until the learner is independently doing the skill.

Modeling

Teaching by showing

Goal
By showing how to do a skill, the learner may be able to learn the skill by copying the actions.

How
Act out a specific skill that you would like the learner to learn (called "modeling" the skill). The learner may independently begin to imitate you, or you might give the instruction "your turn" or "now you try" to encourage them to imitate the same skill.

Context
Modeling is often used in everyday life as a way for individuals to learn new skills. Individuals often learn social skills and self-help skills by watching others' actions. Promote learning new skills by following the modeling steps. If your learner frequently copies peers, family members, or scenes from their favorite shows, this could be a good strategy choice for teaching new skills!

Tip
Video modeling has also been shown to be an effective learning strategy, especially in teaching social skills and play skills. The learner watches a video of someone acting out the skill and then will imitate the skill on their own.

Modeling
Social skills

1

→

Model

Act out the target skill in a situation in which this skill would likely be used.

Here, the teachers are modeling conversation skills while eating dinner.

Modeling
Coping skills

1

→

Model

When the learner is frustrated or angry about something, first model the coping skill that you have been working on teaching.

See visuals, pg. 181

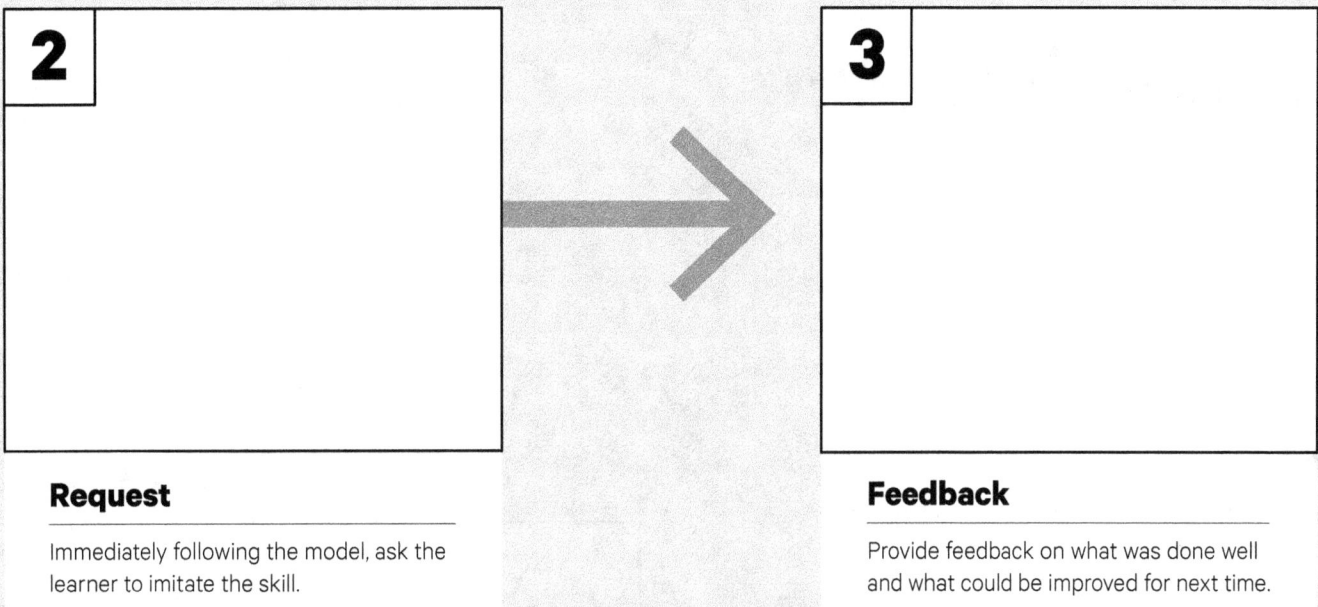

Request

Immediately following the model, ask the learner to imitate the skill.

Feedback

Provide feedback on what was done well and what could be improved for next time.

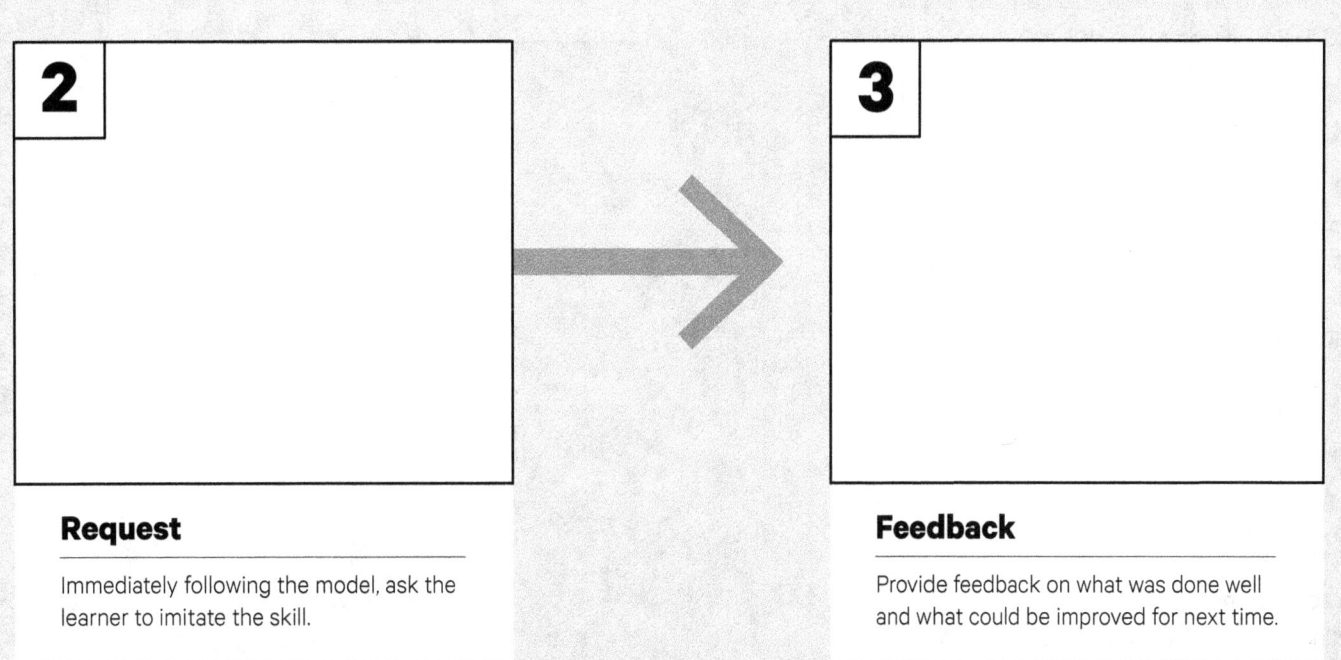

Request

Immediately following the model, ask the learner to imitate the skill.

Feedback

Provide feedback on what was done well and what could be improved for next time.

Generalization

Expanding learning

Goal

Expand learning of one skill in a particular setting (e.g. tying shoes at home) to being able to apply that skill in various settings (e.g. school, park), and in various ways (e.g. different shoes), and with various people. This is called "generalization." The goal is that the skill will emerge in situations that haven't been specifically taught.

How

When teaching a new skill, consider different locations, people, and materials that could be introduced to expand the learning of this skill.

Context

All skills must be generalized in order to say that a learner has "mastered" that skill. Teach and practice the skill in a variety of contexts until the learner can do the skill in novel contexts. For example: teach the learner to answer "what's your name?" with parent, teacher, and sibling. If a peer asks the learner, "what's your name?" and the learner correctly answers, this skill is likely mastered!

Tip

For some learners, first, teach a new skill in a structured setting prior to practicing it in a variety of contexts. For other learners, you can teach in a variety of contexts from the beginning. Think about how your learner learns best!

See visuals, pg. 183

Teach the skill

- With various people
- In various settings
- With various materials
- Using varied language
- At various times of the day

Play Skills

Teaching play skills to improve social relationships

Goal

Assist the learner with progressing through play skill development in order to build their social relationships.

How

- Determine where the learner is currently on the stages of play skill development
- Set the goal as the type of play that is the next stage
- Practice this next stage with the learner by modeling what to do and making play-related comments
- Reinforce the learner's attempts at copying your actions or comments

Context

When teaching play skills, it is helpful to practice the skills with the learner a few times before moving to playing with peers.

When the learner is ready to practice with peers, the teacher can initially assist by modeling what to do and then gradually pull back to let the learners play alone.

Note

There's no wrong way to play, but learning to play different ways expands opportunities for social relationships.

1. Onlooker

The learner is watching peers play, but is not interacting with them or the play materials.

Recommended goals: sustained attention in play alongside a peer, one-step imitation of play actions

4. Pretend play

The learner is using items in creative ways to pretend they are something else or that s/he is someone else.

Recommended goals: tolerating sharing, requesting items or actions during play

See visuals, pg. 185

2. Parallel play

The learner is playing alongside peers and may or may not be completing the same activity. However, they are not engaging with peers.

Recommended goals: sustained engagement in shared-play activity with peer, following play-related one-step instructions

3. Associative play

The learner is playing with the same materials as a peer and may talk to or look at the peer, but they are not working together to complete the activity.

Recommended goals: imitating play-related comments or actions, making reciprocal statements

6. Cooperative play

The learners play a game or an activity together and share a common goal. They use social skills to take turns and talk about the activity.

Recommended goals: tolerating losing, problem solving during play

5. Social play

The learner learns social play skills including sharing and taking turns. The learner may request for items from the peer.

Recommended goals: sustained engagement in turn-taking games, initiating and responding to play-related questions and comments

Joint Attention

The start of social skills: Teaching to share a common interest

Goal

Teach the learner to initiate and respond to shared interests.

How

Joint attention means that two people are attending to the same thing. Through their reactions, they should be able to identify how the other person feels about the shared situation. For some learners, we may need to teach them how to respond to others' requests to attend, as well as how to initiate joint attention themselves (e.g. "look at this!").

Context

Teach and refine these skills in natural and play settings. Choose activities that target building joint attention like cause-and-effect toys or games where you can have big excited or surprised reactions.

Tip

Use exaggerated expressions while interacting with a toy to help the learner learn to use others' faces as a cue for what they are thinking.

Example: a block tower falls over. Make an exaggerated "surprise" face by raising your eyebrows, covering your mouth and saying "uh-oh!" If the learner looks at you, celebrate their joint attention!

With teacher

Responding

Use a preferred toy to gain the attention of the learner. Move the toy around and encourage the learner to follow it with her eye gaze. Pass the toy across your face while you make play-related facial expressions/reactions to help promote the connection between the toy and your emotions.

Initiating

Reinforce any initiations of joint attention from the learner. If the learner points to something, look at it and respond positively.

See visuals, pg. 187

With peers

Responding with peers

Set the learner up for success with their peers by providing preferred toys that they can attend to together. You may need to assist in responding to peers by saying something like, "Look, she has a doll!"

Initiating with peers

Place preferred items/activities between peers to encourage them to play and interact together. You may need to assist in initiating joint attention and sustaining the attention by saying something like, "That looks cool! Show your friend!"

Official title: Mand Training or Functional Communication Training

Teaching to Request

Teaching how to ask for wants/needs

Goal
- Reduce a challenging behavior by teaching the learner a replacement, and more appropriate, way of getting their needs met
- Build communication skills
- Build self-advocacy skills

How
Identify the situations where the learner would have the highest motivation to communicate their needs. Turn these into teaching moments by teaching them how to communicate in that moment. This could be through modeling (using an AAC device, core board, PECS, or sign language), giving a vocal instruction of what they should say, or using a visual card that they can read out loud. If they follow your guidance and communicate, celebrate it! Immediately give them what they requested. If not, give a reminder and one more opportunity to try again.

Context
Requesting is not just about asking for favorite items! Use these steps to teach essential skills such as requesting for more time, requesting help, requesting space, or requesting breaks.

Tip
Consider how your learner learns best! Try using visuals, role plays, and modeling and see which teaching method is most effective for your learner.

1

Identify motivation
Identify what the learner has a motivation to request for: an item, attention, help, etc.

2

Teach
Create an opportunity to teach this skill when there's high motivation. Teach the learner to communicate by modeling the request (AAC device, sign language), giving a vocal instruction (as pictured), or using a visual prompt. Think about how your learner learns best!

See visuals, pg. 189

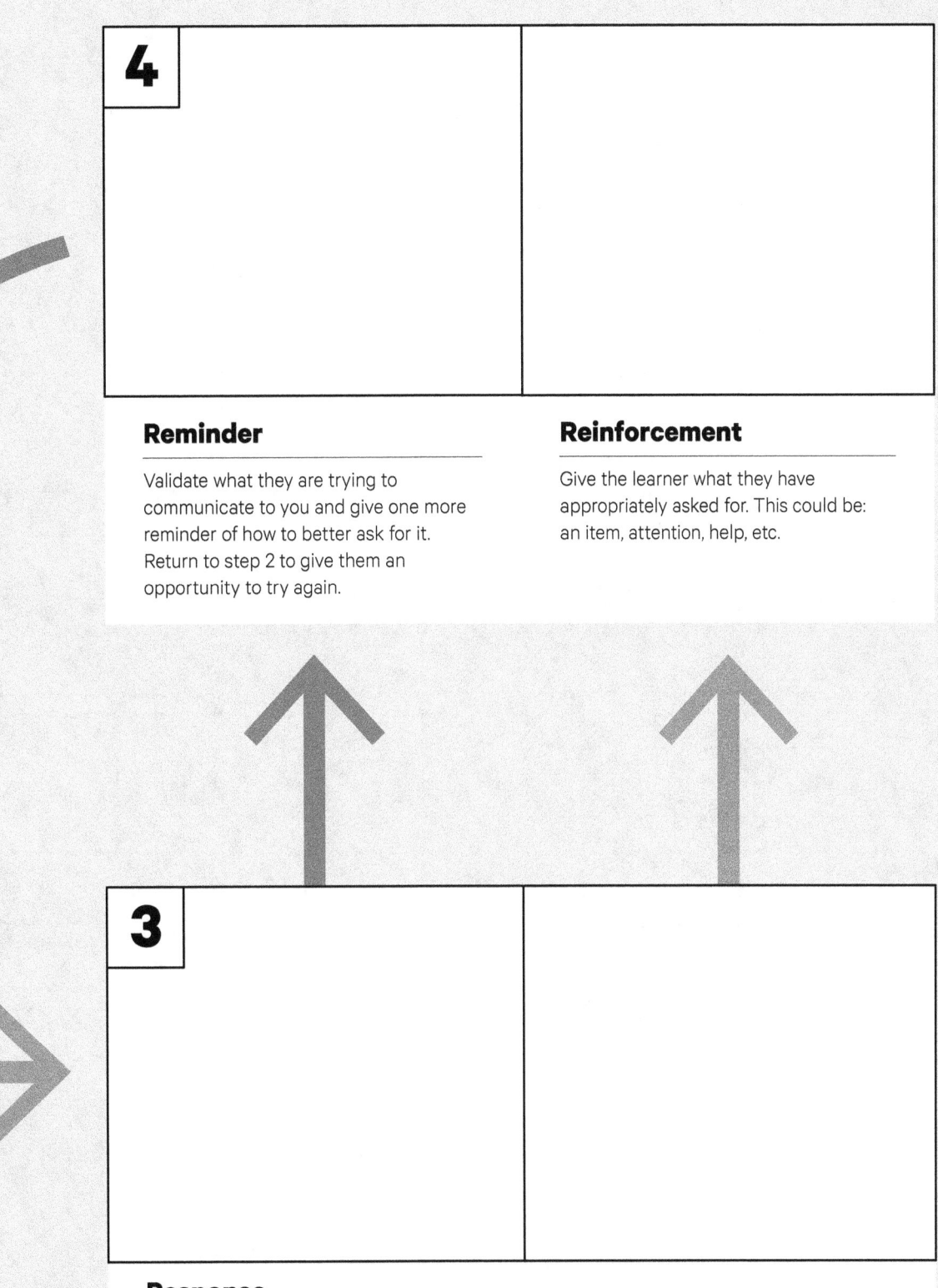

Reminder
Validate what they are trying to communicate to you and give one more reminder of how to better ask for it. Return to step 2 to give them an opportunity to try again.

Reinforcement
Give the learner what they have appropriately asked for. This could be: an item, attention, help, etc.

Response
The learner responds, either by using functional communication or engaging in challenging behaviors in attempt to communicate needs.

Putting it all Together

Turning off Electronics

Goal

Have a structured approach to supporting learners in following through with the instruction of turning off electronics (e.g. iPad, phone, video games, computer).

How

A combination of letting the learner know that this tricky transition is coming up (Priming) and following through with this instruction (Tell, Show, Help) will help to create consistent expectations and more success!

Context

Use these strategies prior to giving the instruction to transition off electronics, to follow through with that instruction, and to celebrate successes! The more consistent you are, the more effective this will be.

Tip

When asking to turn off electronics, try telling the learner to "turn off and put down" rather than "turn off and give to me." For some learners, it's easier if they can control where they put it, rather than having to give it to someone else.

1

Priming (pg. 54)

Prior to giving the instruction to turn off, give a transition warning. You can say, "five more minutes on tablet" or "when you finish that level, it's time to put away tablet."

Note: If your learner is learning to ask for more time as a replacement behavior, now would be a good time to remind them to use their communication skills to request this!

⬇

2

Easy, Easy, Hard (pg. 58)

Use the Easy, Easy, Hard strategy to set them up for success prior to giving the difficult "turn off" instruction. First, give two easier requests relating to the electronic game (e.g. "show me your score!," "tell your friends 'bye'!").

See visuals, pg. 191

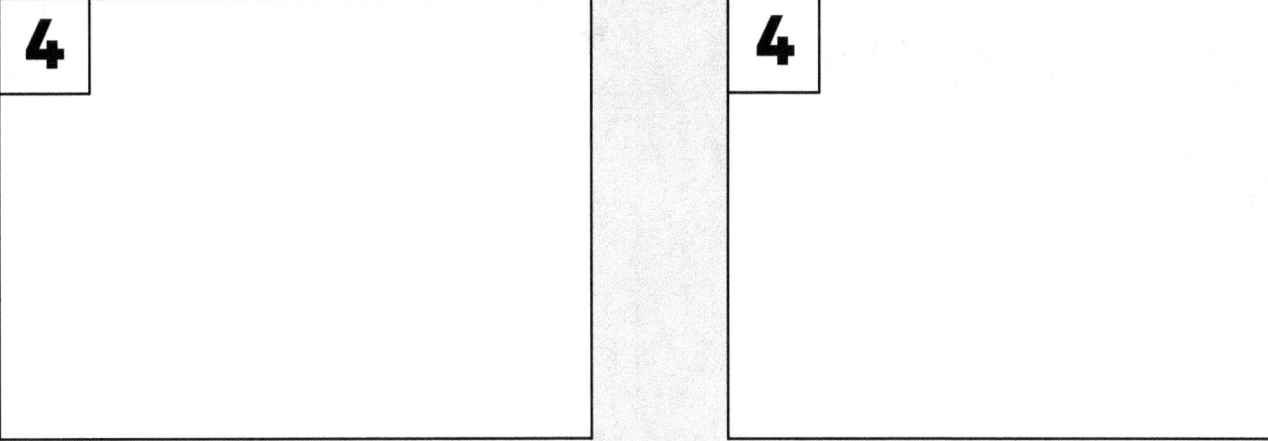

Extinction + Redirection (pg. 76)

Follow through with the instruction by not allowing the learner to continue playing. Move to the 3rd step of Tell, Show, Help where you will help them turn off the device and redirect them to use a coping skill if they are frustrated by this instruction.

Reinforcement (pg. 40)

If the learner follows the instruction and turns off the device, immediately celebrate by giving social praise ("nice job listening!"). Also, it is ideal if the learner can earn electronics again later as a reward for following the instruction.

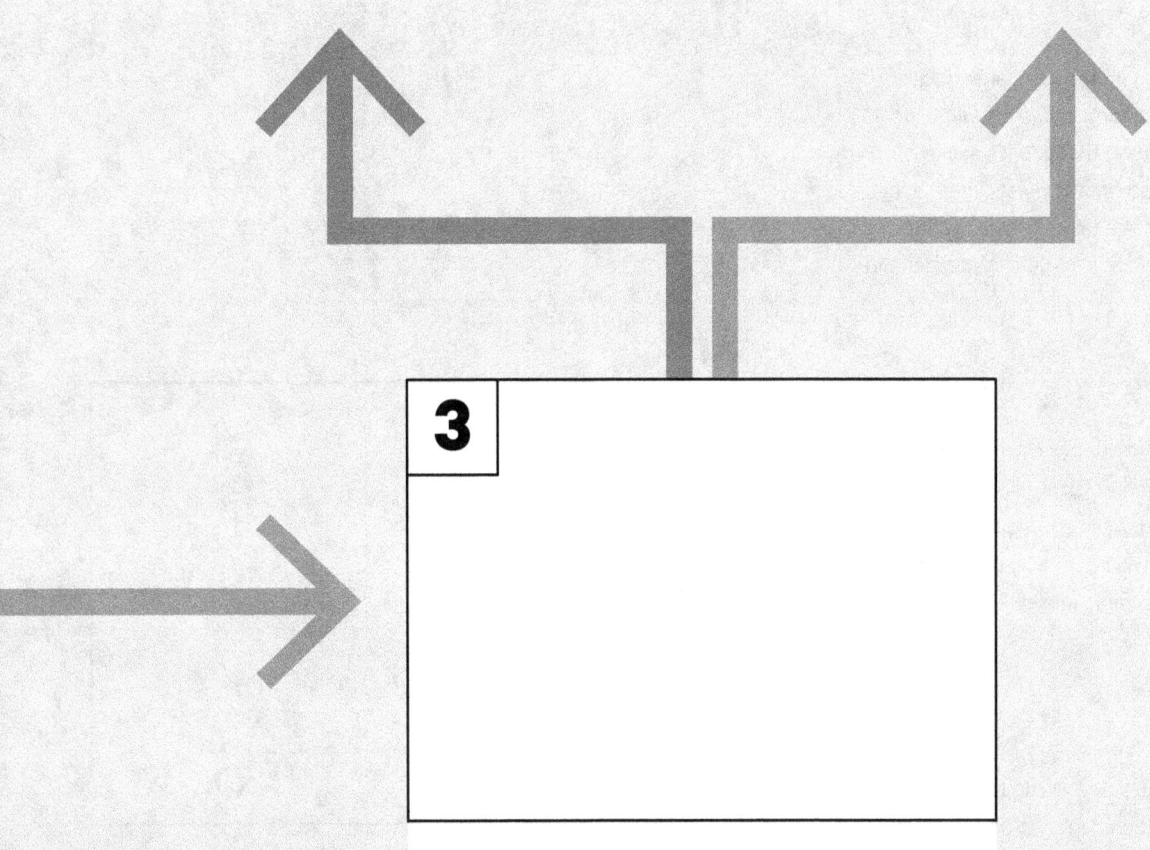

Tell, Show, Help (pg. 66)

Use the Tell, Show, Help strategy to give a clear instruction ("turn off tablet") and follow through.

Here, the teacher is doing the 2nd step by gesturing to the off button.

Improving On-Task Behavior

Goal

Increase the amount of time the learner is on task and the amount of work that is completed.

How

Initiating a task and staying on task is challenging for many learners. In this sequence of strategies, most of the focus is on setting them up for success! Establishing a reward ahead of time (First, Then) and letting them have input on the task (Providing Choices) often helps to build motivation with getting started and completing work.

Context

Consider the tasks that your learner has the most difficulty with starting (whether it's at home or in the classroom). Prioritize using these strategies to support this typically difficult activity and then expand to other tasks when you feel comfortable implementing the strategy package.

Tip

Once the learner is consistently starting tasks with the support of strategies 1-3, focus on shaping the length of time they stay on-task by gradually increasing the expectation of work they need to complete in order to earn the reward.

1

Priming (pg. 54)

Prior to giving the instruction, give a transition warning. This can be in the form of "five more minutes with (preferred item)" or "five more minutes until we do (task)."

2

First, Then (pg. 56)

Use "first, then" language to set clear expectations and clear rewards. The reward could be a favorite item, activity, or just a break away from the task. It might be helpful to use a visual or have the reward nearby. "First (task), then (reward)."

See visuals, pg. 193

4

Extinction + Redirection (pg. 76)
Use Tell, Show, Help strategy to follow through with the instruction. If needed, remind the student to ask for a break or help. Note: If they ask for a break, it should not be as fun as the break they earn for completing the task.

4

Reinforcement (pg. 40)
Provide breaks from the work as a way to reward on-task behavior. Try letting them choose how much work to complete to earn bigger breaks (e.g. "Do you want to do 5 problems, then take a 5 minute break or 10 problems and then take a 10 minute break?").

3

Providing Choices (pg. 60)
Provide a choice relating to the task.
Try offering a choice between:
- Doing front or back of worksheet first
- Doing math or reading task first
- Using crayons or colored pencils
- Having Teacher 1 or Teacher 2 assist

Classroom Disruptions

Goal

Reduce attention-based classroom disruptions by teaching better ways to participate in classroom discussions.

How

Teachers will use proactive strategies to set expectations in their classroom. They will identify learners who may need additional support in learning ways to appropriately participate in class. When disruptions occur, teachers will minimize their reactions and will instead redirect learners to request attention appropriately. When learners do follow the set expectations, teachers will recognize this by immediately providing attention (and possibly additional praise and rewards).

Context

Use these strategies with one target learner or across all learners to prevent and reduce disruptive behaviors in the classroom.

Tip

Combine this strategy with a Whole Class Reward System by setting clear expectations and clear rewards for following these classwide rules during typically disruptive activities.

1

Priming (pg. 54)

Prior to transitioning from a free period to a work period, teacher will inform the class of the expectations for the upcoming activity (e.g. sitting quietly at desk, raising hand to ask/answer questions).

2

Be proactive

Give attention (e.g. calling on them to answer, giving praise) to the target learner(s) at predictable and frequent rates. Gradually increase the time between giving attention. By giving attention at frequent rates, the learner will be less likely to act out in order to try and get attention.

See visuals, pg. 195

4

4

Extinction + Redirection (pg. 76)

Try to minimize reactions to disruptive behaviors. Remain calm and neutral. Recognize nearby students who are following the expectations (peer model) or model what the disruptive student should be doing (raise your own hand as a signal for them to copy you).

Reinforcement (pg. 40)

Immediately following initiation of appropriate behavior (raising hand), reinforce by providing attention (calling on the learner). Following several instances of appropriate behavior, provide additional attention (having the learner come to front of class).

3

Building Better Behaviors (pg. 90)

Provide reinforcement (giving attention) to the learner only following the better way to request attention (e.g. raising hand). Provide attention to other learners who are engaging in appropriate behaviors as a signal of what is expected.

Sharing Toys

Goal

Increase tolerance in waiting for a turn with preferred items to improve social and play skills.

How

Set clear expectations for sharing. Model how to appropriately wait for a turn. After a few successful times sharing, gradually increase the amount of time the learner needs to wait for the item.

Context

Practice these steps during play times when the learner and another person are both interested in playing with the same item. These steps can also be practiced as a role play where the teacher says, "let's practice sharing!" and pretends to be a peer who is interested in the item.

Tip

Some learners may benefit from visuals to help learn the expectations of sharing. Try using timers or visual cards that say "my turn, your turn" to teach this skill in a more structured way.

1

Priming (pg. 54)

Remind learners of expectations while sharing preferred items (e.g. each person gets x amount of minutes, then switch).

2

Modeling (pg. 98)

Model appropriate behavior while waiting for turn: sitting calmly, watching other person, not reaching for item.

See visuals, pg. 197

4

Extinction + Redirection (pg. 76)

Try to prevent attempts to grab the item when it's not their turn. If this happens, remind them of the specific sharing expectations and offer to support in a coping strategy if needed.

4

Reinforcement (pg. 40)

When building sharing skills, we want to recognize and celebrate both waiting for a turn and giving up the item when the turn is over. Consider giving bonus time with the item for successful sharing!

3

Shaping (wait time) (pg. 96)

As the learner practices this skill, gradually increase the amount of time they need to wait for the item.

Picky Eating

Goal
Increase learner's acceptance of new foods.

How
Use First, Then strategy for each bite of food: "First (new food), then (favorite food)." Over time, increase the number of bites of the new food needed to earn the favorite food. If the learner does not accept the bite of the new food, say "that's ok, but no (favorite food)" and end snack time. This low-pressure approach helps take the stress away from picky eating! Try again once the learner requests their favorite food again. *The favorite food must only be given following the learner eating the new food.*

Context
Collaborate with the family and a doctor to create a list of foods that you would like to incorporate into the learner's diet. In addition to nutritional needs, consider what typical dishes are eaten at family meals, as this would increase the learner's involvement in their family culture. Practice this strategy at snack time every day. Once the learner is comfortable eating five bites of a new food before receiving the favorite food, start adding this new food to their usual meal times (e.g. pack it in their lunchbox, serve it with breakfast, etc.).

Tips
Try modeling eating the new food yourself first! By showing that you tried and liked the new food, they may be more open to trying it out for themselves.

1

Identify foods

Create a list of foods that the learner currently likes to eat (these will be the rewards). Create a list of new foods to try.

Note

It's important to consult and collaborate with other professionals and providers to ensure there are no medical barriers causing the picky eating, especially if your learner is having challenges with chewing and swallowing. Consider if sensory sensitivities may also be impacting your learner's diet. If so, try to pick new foods that have similar textures to foods they already are eating.
An Occupational Therapist (OT) would be a great person to collaborate with!

See visuals, pg. 199

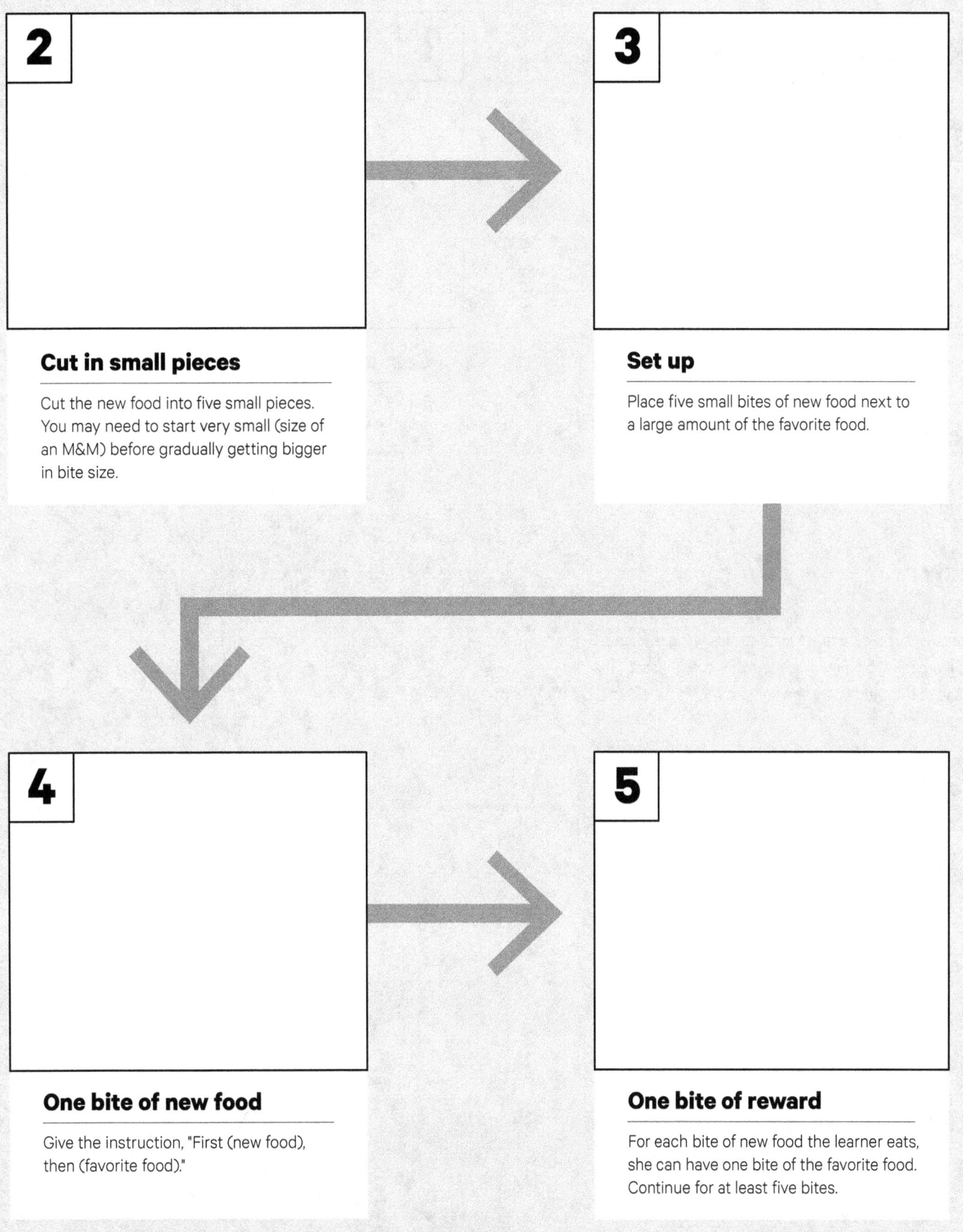

2 Cut in small pieces

Cut the new food into five small pieces. You may need to start very small (size of an M&M) before gradually getting bigger in bite size.

3 Set up

Place five small bites of new food next to a large amount of the favorite food.

4 One bite of new food

Give the instruction, "First (new food), then (favorite food)."

5 One bite of reward

For each bite of new food the learner eats, she can have one bite of the favorite food. Continue for at least five bites.

Following Directions

Goal

Support learners in following directions the first time asked.

How

By giving clear instructions, using an individualized proactive strategy, and consistently following through, the learner will be more likely to follow the direction. Try to use this strategy package consistently to have the greatest impact.

Context

These steps can be used for any instruction but should be used consistently with instructions that are non-preferred or are typically difficult for the learner to follow.

Tip

Make a copy of this visual strategy and place it in settings where the learner typically has trouble following directions (e.g. in their bedroom, at their desk, in the car, etc.) This will help you remember to use the steps during challenging times.

1

Gain attention

Before giving an instruction, make sure to gain the learner's attention. Giving eye contact is not necessary, but it's helpful to come closer to the learner and ensure they're not distracted with another item/activity in that moment.

See visuals, pg. 201

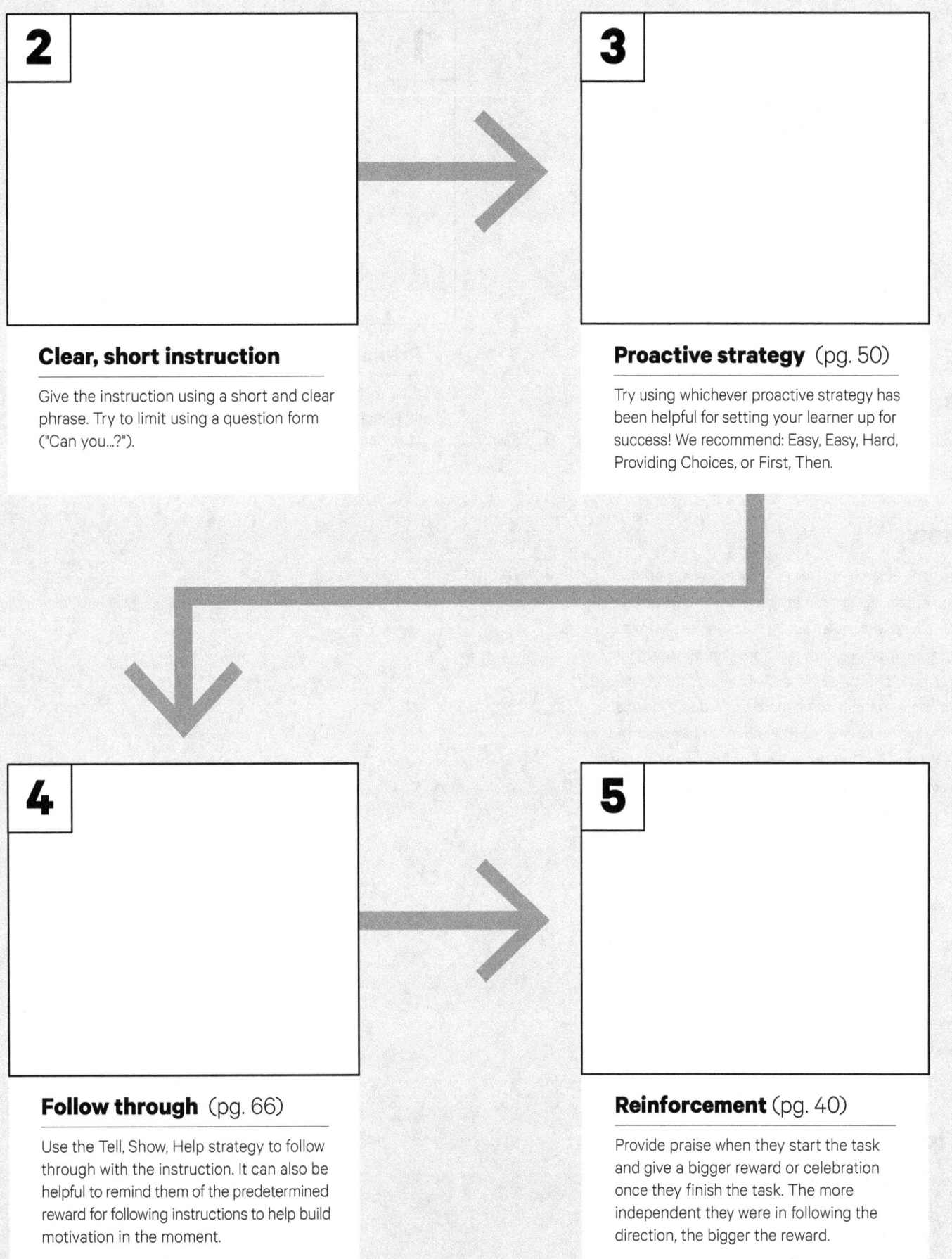

2

Clear, short instruction

Give the instruction using a short and clear phrase. Try to limit using a question form ("Can you...?").

3

Proactive strategy (pg. 50)

Try using whichever proactive strategy has been helpful for setting your learner up for success! We recommend: Easy, Easy, Hard, Providing Choices, or First, Then.

4

Follow through (pg. 66)

Use the Tell, Show, Help strategy to follow through with the instruction. It can also be helpful to remind them of the predetermined reward for following instructions to help build motivation in the moment.

5

Reinforcement (pg. 40)

Provide praise when they start the task and give a bigger reward or celebration once they finish the task. The more independent they were in following the direction, the bigger the reward.

Transitions

Goal
Create smoother transitions from preferred activities to non-preferred activities.

How
Transitions are tricky! You are asking a learner to stop engaging with something fun and start doing something less preferred. By preparing the learner in advance, it's more likely the transition will be smooth. Priming is often a very effective strategy for transitions, but some learners may benefit from adding in another proactive strategy once it's time to actually start the transition (like Easy, Easy, Hard or Providing Choices). Make sure you follow through once the transition instruction is given and don't forget to celebrate moments of success!

Context
Use these steps when there is an expectation for the learner to transition from a highly preferred task (e.g. recess, free play at home, watching TV, playing on electronics, playing with friends) to a less-preferred task (e.g. classwork/homework, chores, going somewhere in the car).

Tip
Some learners may benefit from using a timer to signal an upcoming transition. Try having them press "start" on the timer themselves or having the timer where they can easily see it to maximize their acknowledgement of the remaining time prior to the transition instruction.

1

Prime 1 (pg. 54)
Prior to a transition that may be challenging for the learner, give a 'prime' of what change is upcoming.

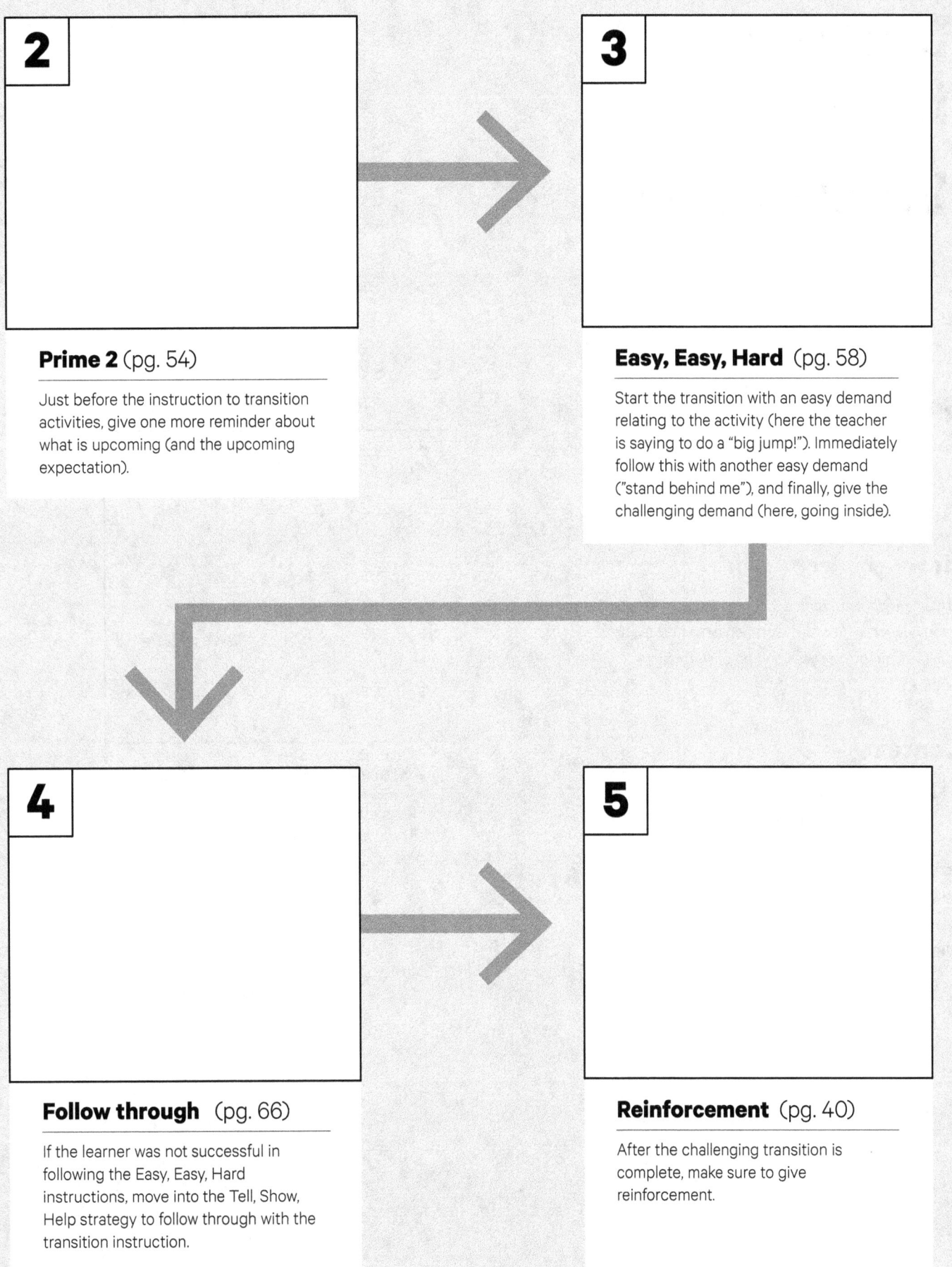

See visuals, pg. 203

Prime 2 (pg. 54)

Just before the instruction to transition activities, give one more reminder about what is upcoming (and the upcoming expectation).

Easy, Easy, Hard (pg. 58)

Start the transition with an easy demand relating to the activity (here the teacher is saying to do a "big jump!"). Immediately follow this with another easy demand ("stand behind me"), and finally, give the challenging demand (here, going inside).

Follow through (pg. 66)

If the learner was not successful in following the Easy, Easy, Hard instructions, move into the Tell, Show, Help strategy to follow through with the transition instruction.

Reinforcement (pg. 40)

After the challenging transition is complete, make sure to give reinforcement.

Learning Personal Information

Goal

Assist the learner in learning important personal information: name, age, birthday, address, phone number and parents' names.

How

Use a variety of strategies that are effective ways to teach new skills. Adjust the strategies to fit the learner's skill level and preferences and practice through repetition.

Context

It is important for individuals to know their personal information as a safety precaution.

Learning this information may require substantial teaching effort and repetition, but the use of these strategies will help the learner initially learn and remember the information more quickly.

Personalized Teaching (pg. 88)

Find natural opportunities to practice answering the questions. The more practice, the better.

See visuals, pg. 205

1

Shaping (pg. 96)

Start small and build the learner's answer over time. This is especially relevant for longer answers like phone numbers and addresses. Teach just a few numbers at a time.

2

Modeling (pg. 98)

Show the learner how to answer the question correctly, either through verbally saying the answer or writing the answer down (whichever way the learner learns better).

3

Generalization (pg. 100)

Once the learner is making progress with answering the question, have other people ask the question. This will ensure the learner can still answer correctly when a new person asks.

Encouraging Communication

Note
This strategy is from our book, *AAC Visualized*, which teaches strategies for supporting learners who are nonvocal or have limited communication skills.

Goal
Encourage the use of communication (regardless of mode) for learners who are nonvocal or have limited language skills.

How
Choose one word each week to model throughout the day in a variety of contexts, teaching the concept of that word. Model using their communication method (e.g. vocal, sign language, AAC device, core board, PECS, etc.). Here, there's no expectation for the learner to communicate just yet, but instead they are learning by watching. As you speak in full sentences, emphasize just the chosen word of the week by pointing to it on the core board or AAC device. Next, you'll create an opportunity where they should be motivated to communicate; then you'll do a dramatic pause signaling it's their turn to join in. Because you've been modeling this word so often, they hopefully will be able to communicate using that word in this moment! Check out *AAC Visualized* for more step-by-step strategies for introducing and expanding communication skills.

Context
Use this strategy with those who are just starting to learn a communication method. The more you model, the better. Get everyone on board!

Legend
- Vocal
- ASL
- AAC device & Core board

Bold text: Core words

Standard text: Fringe words

See visuals, pg. 207

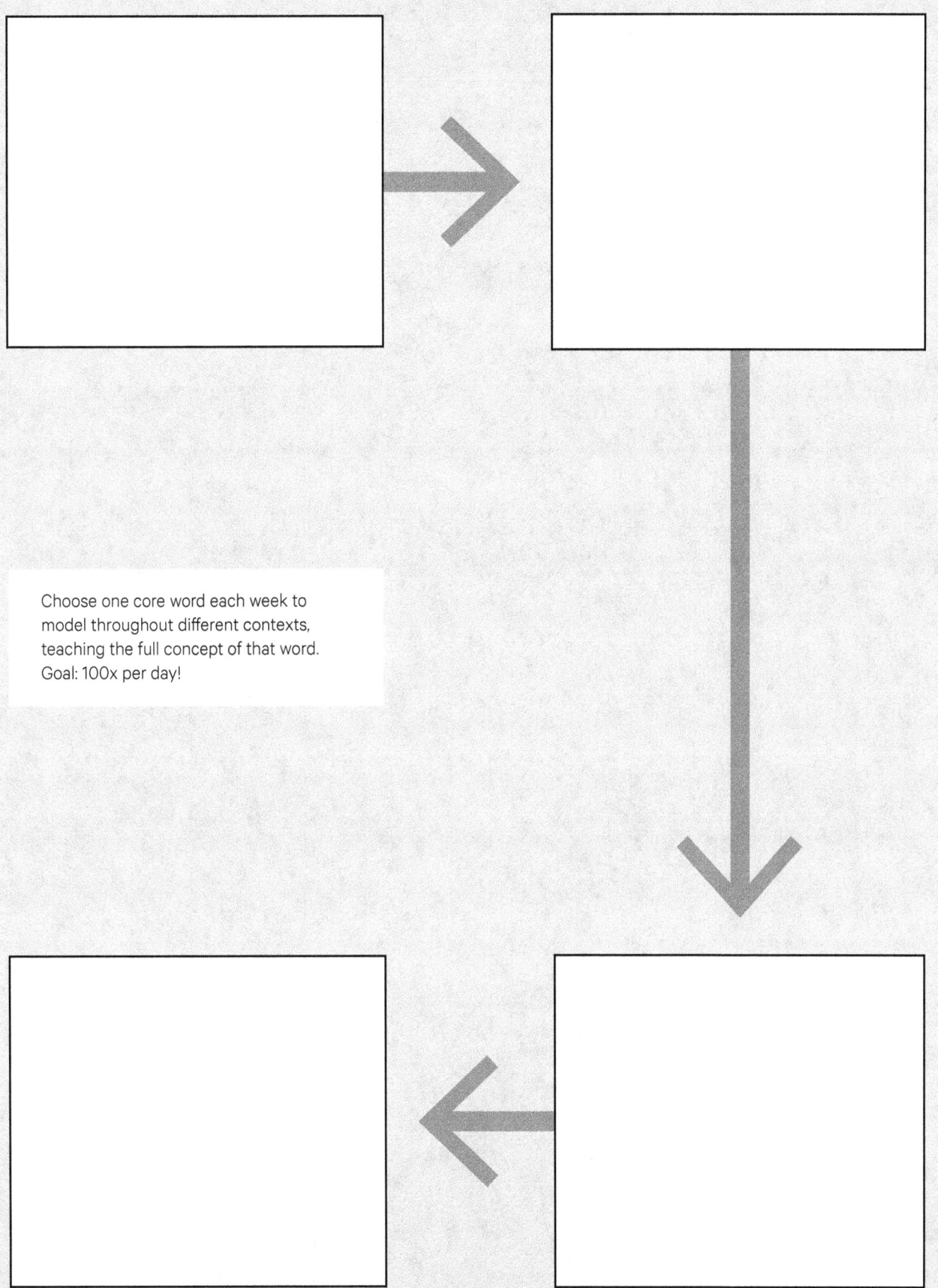

Choose one core word each week to model throughout different contexts, teaching the full concept of that word. Goal: 100x per day!

Strategies for an Inclusive Classroom

Official title: Group Contingency

Whole Class Reward System

Building and rewarding better classroom behaviors

Goal

Build specific skills for the whole group during a typical teaching lesson.

How

Set and teach 3-5 defined classwide expectations relating to skills that you want to build. Have your learners share ideas for rewards to earn, then split them up into teams, and choose an activity that your learners struggle with the most. Give points for following expectations; the group with most points wins!

Context

Use this strategy when you can clearly identify the hardest part of your day (e.g. read-alouds, small groups, walking in the halls). Whole class reward systems are helpful for learners of all ages and in any setting.

Tip

Try using an app like Class DoJo to electronically track points. The students can create their own characters to engage them even further. Another tip is to utilize student helpers who can help with recognizing peers who are engaging in the expected behaviors and assisting the teacher in giving out points. Research shows that this helps recognize and reward positive behaviors but also reduces challenging behaviors in the student helpers, as they are busy with their assigned job!

1 Set expectations

Choose 1-3 positively-worded behavior expectations for the entire class. Introduce the expectations to the students and hang up a visual in front of the class.

4 Choose activity

Identify an activity when challenging behaviors most often occur. For this teacher, whole class attending at story time is often challenging.

See visuals, pg. 209

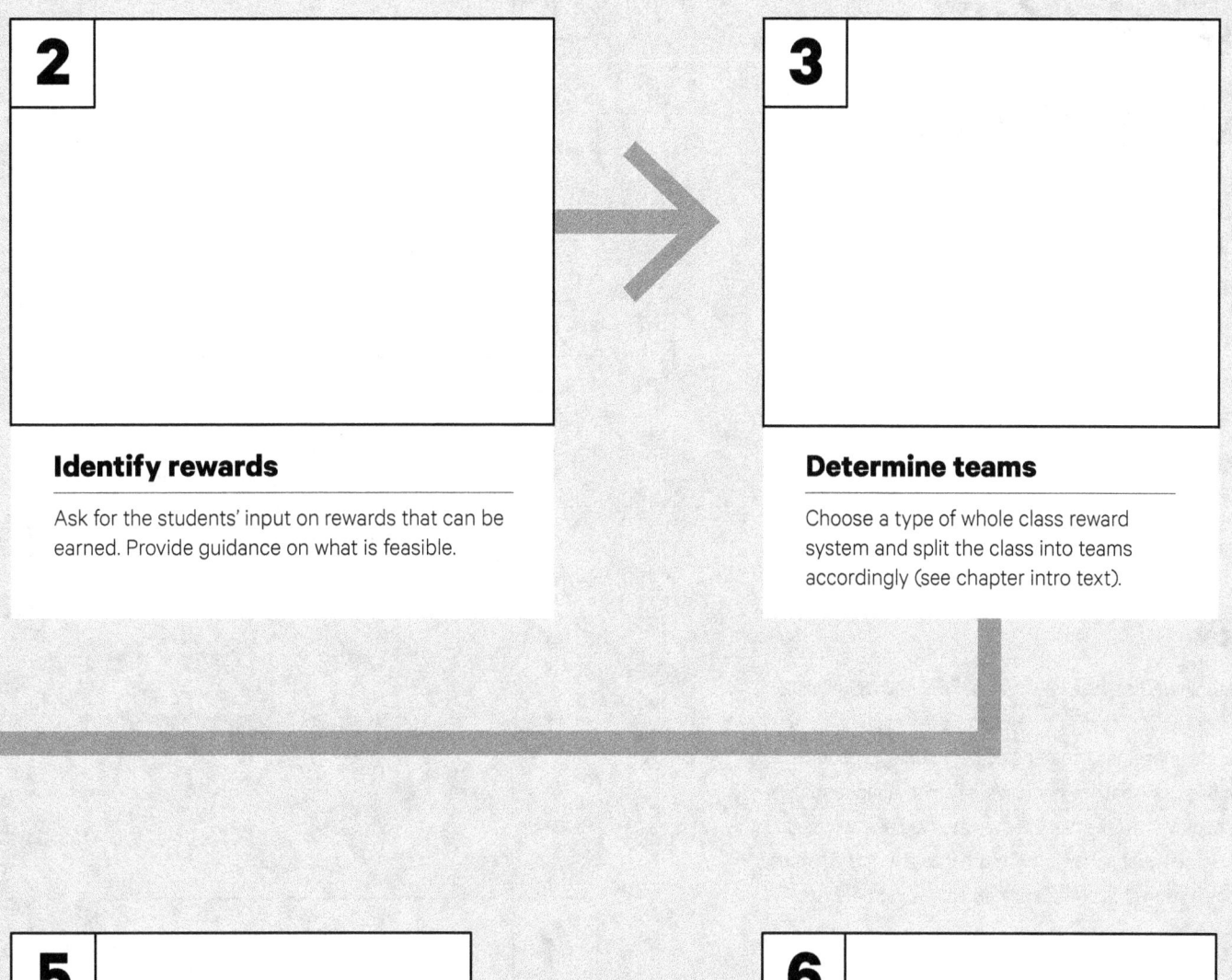

2

Identify rewards

Ask for the students' input on rewards that can be earned. Provide guidance on what is feasible.

3

Determine teams

Choose a type of whole class reward system and split the class into teams accordingly (see chapter intro text).

5

Play!

Each day during this particular activity, give points to students or teams who engage in the target expectations.

6

Reward

When students or teams have met the expectations, they win the reward!

Check-in, Check-out

Frequent feedback meetings throughout the day

Goal

Improve a specific learner's behaviors by giving frequent reminders of expectations and feedback.

How

Determine 1-3 positively-worded behavior expectations for the learner. Set the check-in schedule based on how often they are engaging in challenging behaviors. Collaborate with the family and learner to identify motivating rewards. At check-ins, the teacher will evaluate progress and remind the learner what behaviors will earn their rewards. Rewards will be given at the predetermined time (at home or at school).

Context

This strategy is helpful for individual learners who exhibit consistent challenging behaviors throughout the school day. It's especially effective for learners who value adult attention, as they will be having brief 1:1 interactions throughout the day.

Tip

Build independence with accountability by having the learner reflect on if they earned their points or not during each check-in. You can also decide to give bonus rewards for honesty when introducing this expectation.

1

Set expectations

Choose 1-3 positively-worded behavior expectations specific to this learner. Introduce the system by teaching them these daily expectations. Use the visual provided in the "Tools" chapter!

4

Check-in

At the beginning of each school day and at the scheduled check-in times, the teacher will remind the learner of the expectations and what rewards are available for following these expectations.

See visuals, pg. 211

2

Set schedule

Determine how often the target challenging behavior is occurring (about every x minutes). Set up your check-in schedule to have feedback meetings just a little bit prior (e.g. set your meetings to occur every 30 minutes if the behaviors happen about every 35 minutes).

3

Set rewards

Collaborate with the family and learner to identify motivating rewards. The team may choose to give smaller rewards throughout the day (at check-in times) or a bigger reward at the end of the day (at school or at home).

5

Check-out

During the scheduled check-ins throughout the day, the teacher and learner will evaluate together if the learner followed the expectations during that previous period. At the end of the day, they will review the whole day's behavior and determine if the reward was earned.

6

Reward

The learner will bring the paper home with them to share with their family. If they earned the reward that day, the family will immediately give it when the learner arrives home.

Official title: Point system

Individual Points Plan

Discrete individual support to build motivation

Goal
Build specific skills for an individual by recognizing and rewarding these behaviors.

How
Establish a long-term goal and consider their current levels of skills needed to meet this goal. Determine 1-3 specific skills that will help the learner achieve the long-term goal. Collaborate with the learner to determine rewards and how many points are needed to earn each reward. Throughout the day, discretely give points when the learner engages in one of the target skills. Once determined points are earned, the learner receives the reward.

Context
This strategy is helpful for individual learners who struggle with motivation to complete standard academic and behavior expectations. Learners will need to be able to sustain waiting for their rewards for this strategy to be effective.

Tip
If the learner has not earned enough points to earn a reward within the first 3 days, adjust the points plan to make it more attainable by changing either the amount of points needed or when the rewards are given (e.g. end of day vs. half day).

1

Set expectations
Choose 1-3 positively-worded behavior expectations specific to this learner. Introduce the system by teaching them these daily expectations. Use the visual provided in the "Tools" chapter!

4

Check-in
At the beginning of each school day and at the scheduled check-in times, the teacher will remind the learner of the expectations and what rewards are available for following these expectations.

See visuals, pg. 213

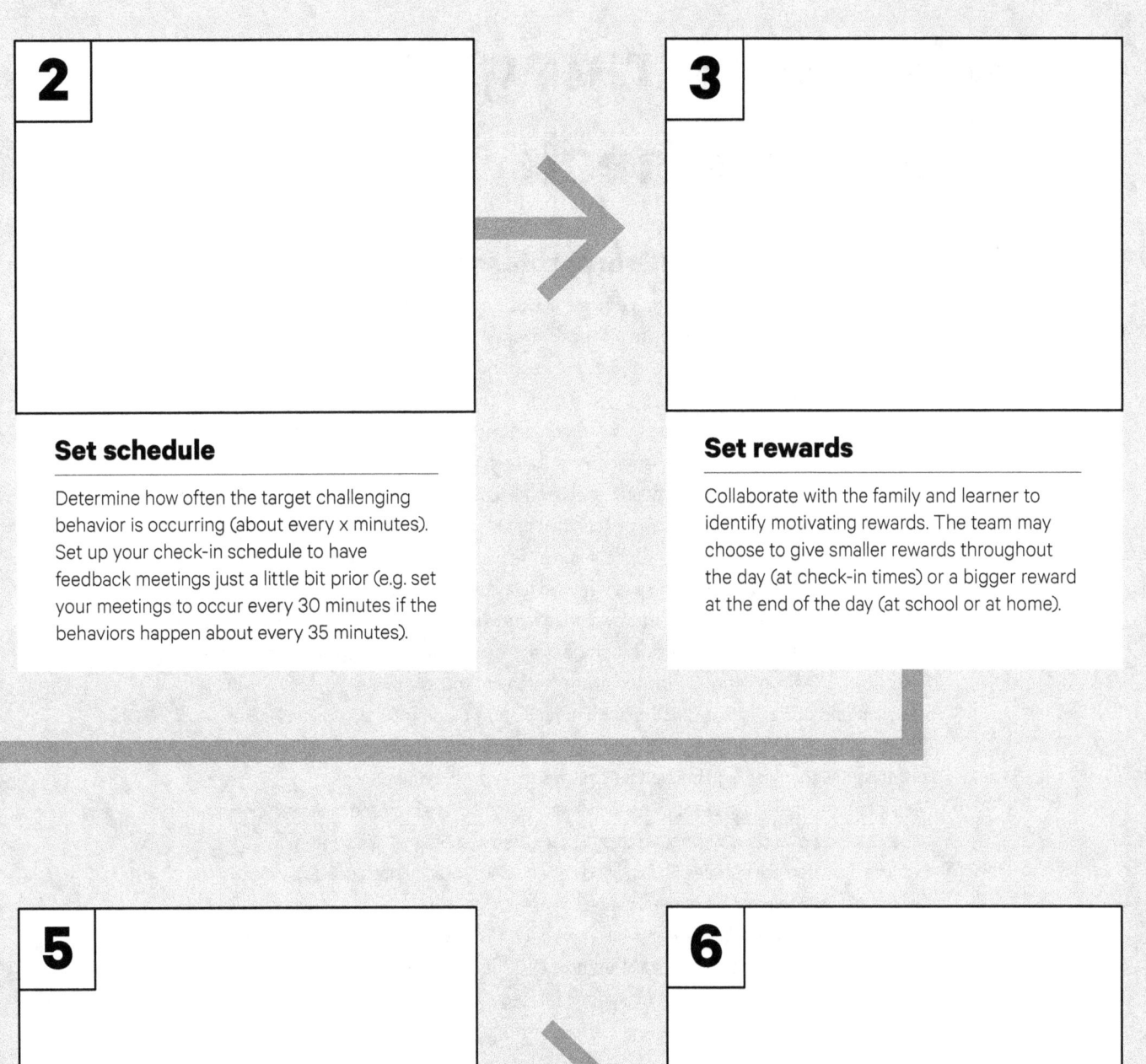

Set schedule

Determine how often the target challenging behavior is occurring (about every x minutes). Set up your check-in schedule to have feedback meetings just a little bit prior (e.g. set your meetings to occur every 30 minutes if the behaviors happen about every 35 minutes).

Set rewards

Collaborate with the family and learner to identify motivating rewards. The team may choose to give smaller rewards throughout the day (at check-in times) or a bigger reward at the end of the day (at school or at home).

Check-out

During the scheduled check-ins throughout the day, the teacher and learner will evaluate together if the learner followed the expectations during that previous period. At the end of the day, they will review the whole day's behavior and determine if the reward was earned.

Reward

The learner will bring the paper home with them to share with their family. If they earned the reward that day, the family will immediately give it when the learner arrives home.

Behavior Strategies Learning Check

For ABA providers and paraprofessionals

- [ ] Describe and demonstrate 3 proactive strategies using approachable language, including the goal, how, and context as it relates to a specific client
- [ ] Describe and demonstrate 2 strategies for responding to challenging behaviors using approachable language, including the goal, how, and context as it relates to a specific client
- [ ] Describe and demonstrate 2 strategies for reinforcing appropriate behaviors using approachable language, including the goal, how, and context as it relates to a specific client
- [ ] When provided a client-specific scenario, explain and demonstrate what Extinction + Redirection would look like and why this is more ethical than implementing Extinction alone
- [ ] Describe and demonstrate 2 options for differential reinforcement using approachable language, including the goal, how, and context as it relates to a specific client
- [ ] Demonstrate demand-free, child-led play for 5 minutes with a client (Rapport Building strategy)
- [ ] When provided a client's skill acquisition goal, explain how this skill could be taught using Personalized Teaching considering the client's interests and strengths
- [ ] Describe and demonstrate functional communication training (Building Better Behaviors, Teaching to Request strategies, Expanding Communication) using approachable language, including the goal, how, and context as it relates to a specific client
- [ ] Demonstrate supporting a client with a daily living skill through a provided task analysis, showing understanding of various prompting techniques (Breaking Down Skills strategy)
- [ ] Describe the difference between Shaping and Fading using skill acquisition goals specific to a client
- [ ] Describe 3 ways to promote generalization
- [ ] When provided with a client's Behavior Intervention Plan (BIP), demonstrate each strategy during role-play, then with the client (Putting it all Together)
- [ ] When provided with an inclusive classroom strategy, describe how you could support the teacher in implementing the plan

For parents and caregivers

- [ ] After being taught a proactive strategy specific to your family, describe and demonstrate the strategy with your child
- [ ] After being taught a strategy for responding to challenging behaviors specific to your family, describe and demonstrate the strategy with your child
- [ ] After being taught a strategy for recognizing and rewarding appropriate behaviors specific to your family, describe and demonstrate the strategy with your child
- [ ] Demonstrate demand-free, child-led play for 5 minutes (Rapport Building strategy)
- [ ] Demonstrate how to proactively teach communication with your child (Building Better Behaviors, Teaching to Request strategies, Expanding Communication)

- [ ] Demonstrate supporting your child with a daily living skill through a provided task analysis
- [ ] For a specific scenario that is challenging for your child, demonstrate each strategy during role-play, then with your child (Putting it all Together)

For teachers

- [ ] After being taught a proactive strategy specific to your classroom, demonstrate the strategy with your students
- [ ] After being taught a strategy for responding to challenging behaviors specific to your classroom, demonstrate the strategy with your students
- [ ] After being taught a strategy for recognizing and rewarding appropriate behaviors specific to your classroom, demonstrate the strategy with your students
- [ ] Demonstrate demand-free, child-led play for 5 minutes with a student (Rapport Building strategy)
- [ ] Demonstrate how to proactively teach communication with a student (Building Better Behaviors, Teaching to Request strategies, Expanding Communication)
- [ ] For a specific scenario that is challenging for a student, demonstrate each strategy during role-play, then with the student (Putting it all Together)
- [ ] In collaboration with the trainer, explain how to set up and implement a Whole Class Reward System that aligns with your classroom needs
- [ ] In collaboration with the trainer, explain how to set up and implement either the Check-in, Check-out or Individual Points Plan strategy for a specific student

Visuals

See Altering the Environment, pg. 52

See Priming, pg. 54

See First, Then, pg. 56

See Easy, Easy, Hard, pg. 58

See Providing Choices, pg. 60

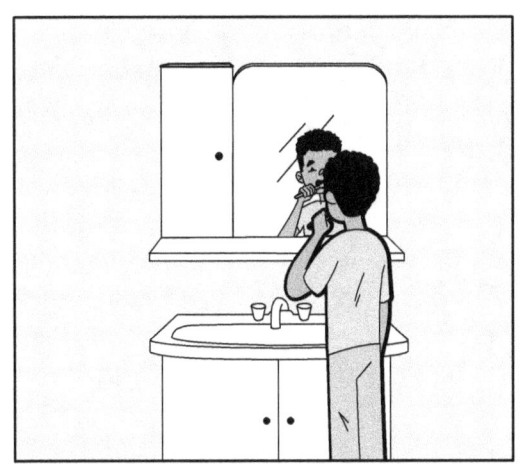

See A Better Way to Say "No", pg. 62

See Tell, Show, Help, pg. 66

See Token Boards, pg. 68

See Extinction by Function, pg. 72

See Extinction by Function, pg. 74

See Extinction + Redirection, pg. 76

See Blocking Unsafe Behaviors, pg. 78

See Managing Self-injurious Behaviors, pg. 80

See 3 Reward Options, pg. 82

167

See Rapport Building, pg. 86

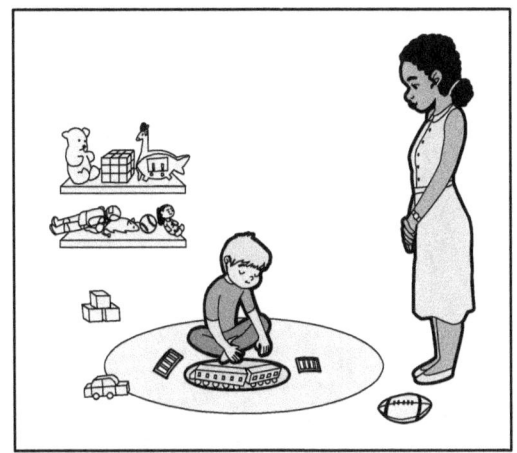

See Personalized Teaching, pg. 88

See Building Better Behaviors, pg. 90

See Breaking Down Skills, pg. 92

See Problem-Solving, pg. 94

See Shaping & Fading, pg. 96

See Modeling, pg. 98

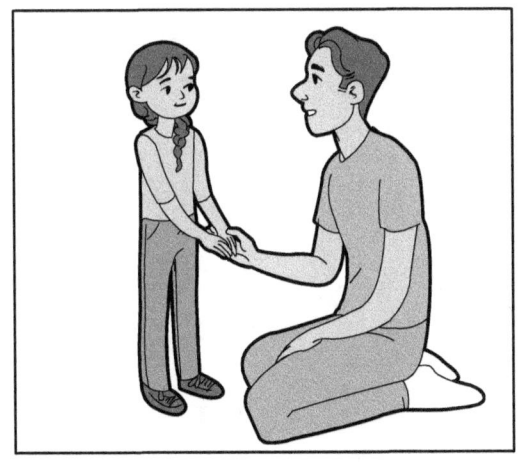

See Generalization, pg. 100

See Play Skills, pg. 102

See Joint Attention, pg. 104

See Teaching to Request, pg. 106

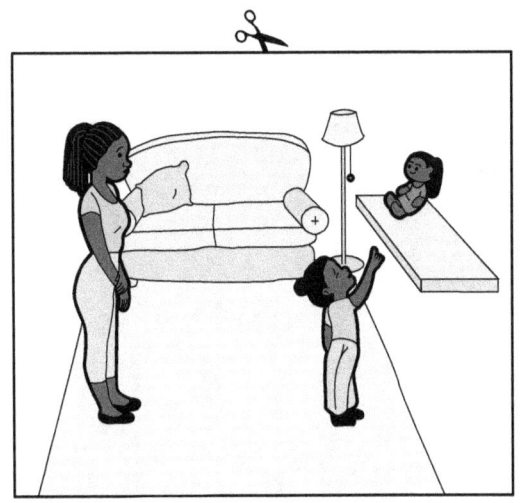

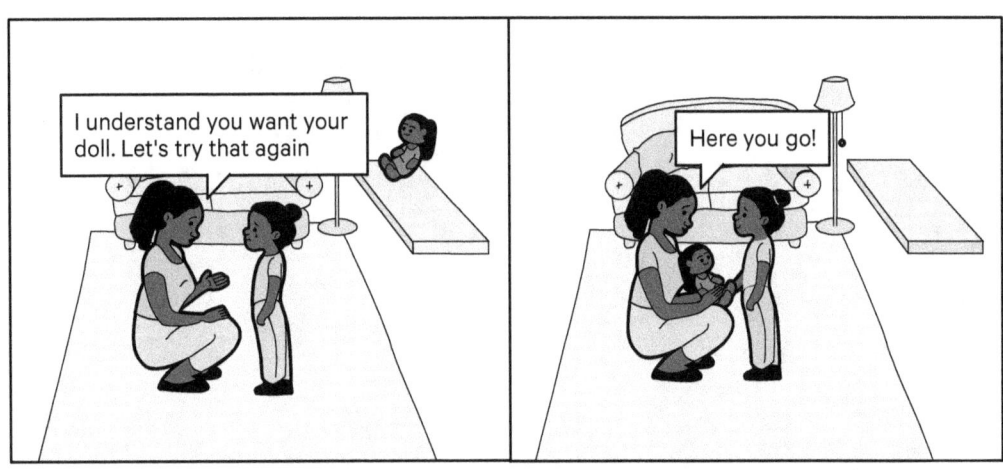

See Turning off Electronics, pg. 110

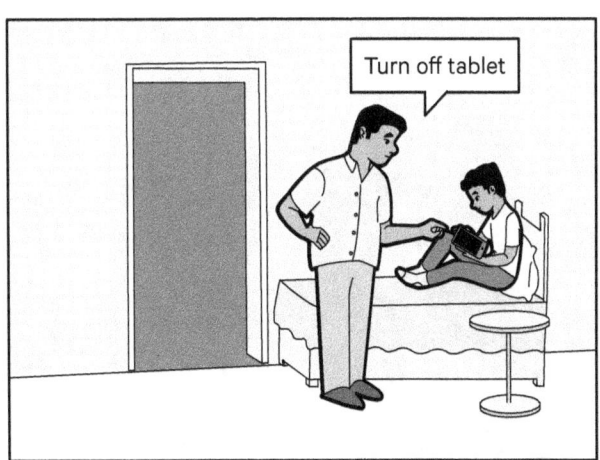

See Improving On-Task Behavior, pg. 112

See Classroom Disruptions, pg. 114

See Sharing Toys, pg. 116

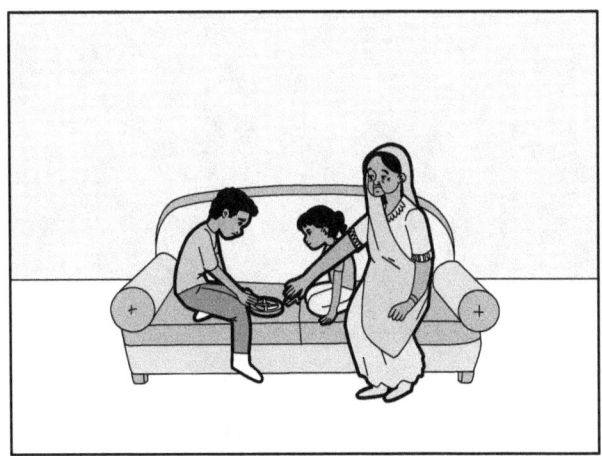

See Picky Eating, pg. 118

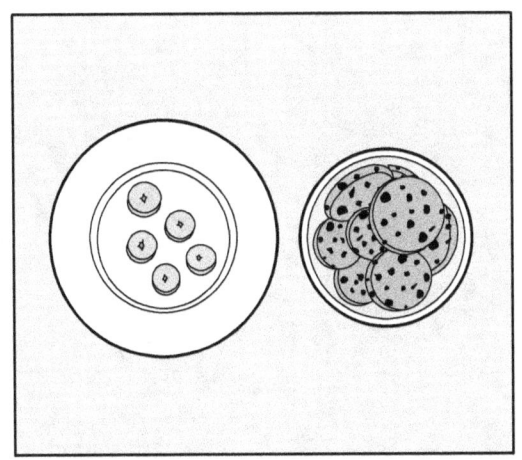
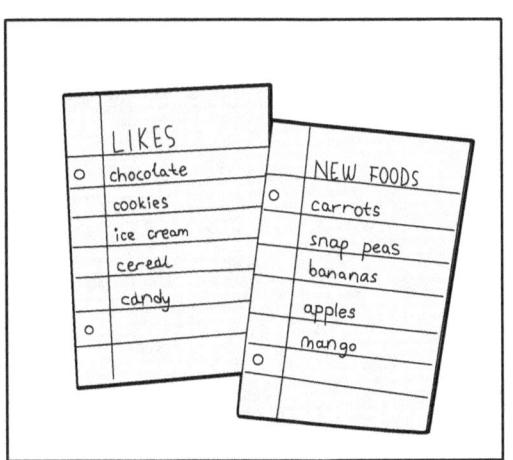
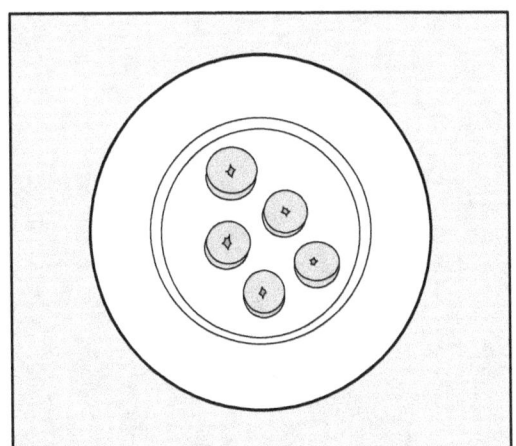

See Following Directions, pg. 120

See Transitions, pg. 122

See Learning Personal Information, pg. 124

See Encouraging Communication, pg. 126

See Whole Class Reward System, pg. 130

See Check-in, Check-out, pg. 132

See Individual Points Plan, pg. 134

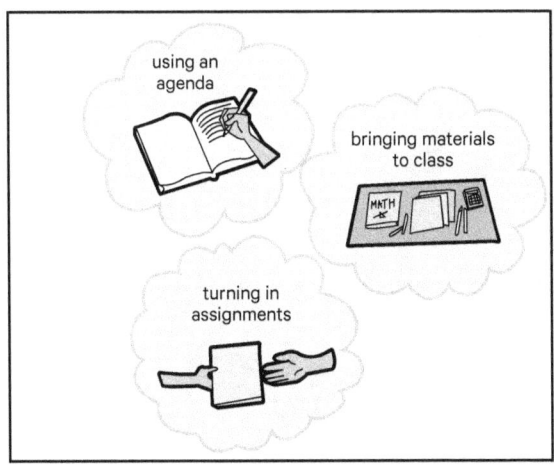
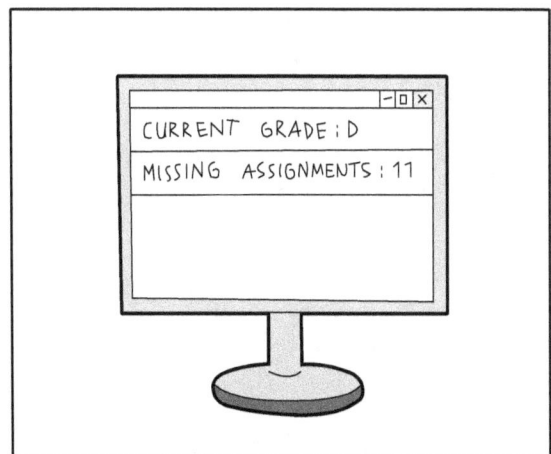